STAIN REMOVAL GUIDE FOR STONE

Frederick M. Hueston

D1566431

BNP
Business News Publishing Company
Troy, Michigan

Library of Congress Cataloging in Publication Data

Hueston, Frederick M.
    Stain removal guide for stone / Frederick M. Hueston
        p. cm.
    ISBN 1-885863-04-7
    1. Building stones--Cleaning. 2. Spotting (Cleaning)
I. Title.
    TH5520.H84   1995   94-23814
    693'.1--dc20   CIP

Administrative Editor: Joanna Turpin
Editors: John Sailer, Michael Reis
Art Director: Mark Leibold
Copy Editor: Carolyn Thompson

This book was written as a general guide. The author and publisher have
neither liability nor can they be responsible to any person or entity for any
misunderstanding, misuse, or misapplication that would cause loss or
damage of any kind, including loss of rights, material, or personal injury,
or alleged to be caused directly or indirectly by the information contained
in this book.

Printed in the United States of America
7 6 5 4 3 2 1

ABOUT THE AUTHOR

Frederick M. Hueston is a certified stone restoration specialist and architectural conservator. His company, National Marble and Stone Consultants, Inc. of Winter Park, FL, offers stain removal as well as a variety of other stone restoration services.

TABLE OF CONTENTS

CHAPTER 1

STAIN IDENTIFICATION AND REMOVAL

Magic Marker™ on a white marble floor. Wine stains after a party. Rust from a filing cabinet. Copper stains from a fountain basin. Oil spots from a leaky forklift. Kool-Aid™ spilled on a countertop. Do we have a problem?

Staining of stone and other porous surfaces can be a major problem unless you have the knowledge of what it takes to remove the stain. The art of stain removal is not difficult if you have the proper tools and, of course, the know-how. This guide is designed to help you remove the most difficult stains by giving you the knowledge and the tools necessary.

Before removing any stain, the reason why stone stains must be understood. The answer to this question is fairly straightforward — stone stains because it is porous. The porous nature of stone allows fluids to enter the stone and become embedded below the surface. The size of the pores determines what will enter the stone and become embedded, and some stones are more porous than others. Honed and textured stone surfaces usually are more porous than polished surfaces. For this reason, a honed or textured stone will have a tendency to absorb more of the staining material.

The longer the stain remains in the stone the deeper it penetrates and the more permanent the stain becomes.

Certain chemical reactions can also take place between the stone and the staining material, permanently setting the stain. This is one reason why it is important to remove a stain as soon as it occurs. A stain is removed by reversing the staining process. In other words, something that is more porous than the stained stone must be used. The stain can literally be sucked back out and into the more porous material. This porous material is known as a *poultice*. Later in this chapter, poulticing will be presented in more detail.

DETERMINING FACTORS

The art of stain removal involves first identifying the stained material, determining its type, and then choosing the proper chemicals and poultice material to remove the stain. This sounds simple enough but sometimes is very difficult. There are many factors that determine if a stain can be removed and how long it will take to remove.

The Stain Itself

Certain stains become very difficult to remove because of their chemical nature. If you have ever tried to remove Magic Marker™ ink from clothing, you know how difficult it can be. On the other hand, certain food stains, although they may look bad, usually are fairly easy to remove. The chapters that follow will describe how to classify certain stains and the difficulty in removing them.

The Age of the Stain

This will provide an indication of what it will take to remove the stain. The following story illustrates this point.

I received a call one afternoon from a homeowner who was quite upset with her remodeler. Apparently, the remodeler had used a black permanent marker on a white marble floor to mark were he was going to place a wall.

When the wall was finally constructed, it was decided that the wall should be moved approximately 2 in. back from the marked area. This of course left a long black line parallel to the wall. When I asked the customer how long the mark had been there she told me approximately 30 days. The remodeler, who was also present, told me he did not understand why the marker would not come off. He said he first tested the marker by placing a mark on the floor and immediately wiping it off. What the remodeler failed to realize is that the ink from the marker slowly penetrated into the stone. I knew right away that this was going to be a difficult task, but I was still successful at removing the marker. It took several applications of poultice, but it worked. If at all possible, try to determine how long the stain has been there. This will give you a good indication of how difficult it will be to remove.

The Size of the Stain

How much of the stone is stained? This will have a major influence on how long it will take to remove the stain. A small area that has been stained with a few drops of oil is going to take a lot less time than an area that has had several gallons of oil spilled on it. It is important to get a general idea, if possible, of how much of the stain has penetrated the stone. I have seen several examples where there was so much material spilled on the floor that it soaked all the way through the stone and into the setting bed below. In this case, it was nearly impossible to remove all of the stain.

Proper Selection of Poultice and Chemical Cleaners

While this may sound quite obvious, the improper selection of chemicals and poultice can either make a stain worse or permanent. Rust or iron is probably one of the most difficult stains to remove. It is important to know which chemicals to use on iron stains. The wrong chemical can oxidize iron to rust and cause permanent staining that will actually become part of the stone. One chemical that will rapidly oxidize iron to rust is common household bleach. I have seen numerous examples where bleach was used in an attempt to remove a rust stain, and it only made matters worse. The stain became darker and larger and was permanently set into the stone. Be careful when choosing chemicals for stain removal.

STAIN IDENTIFICATION

Before any stain can be removed, it is extremely important to find out what the stain is. There are several reasons for this proper stain identification. For example, if the stain is unknown and you try to remove it, you may be using chemicals that will not work or, even worse, may actually set the stain and make it permanent.

So how do you identify stains? The first task is to determine if it is a stain. While this may sound like common sense, there are many problems associated with certain stones that may look like stains but are not. Almost all polished marble will become discolored and dull when it comes in contact with acids. Acids can be found in orange juice, lemons, soft drinks, foods, household and commercial cleaners, bathroom cleaners, etc. This dulling effect caused by acids is a condition known as *etching*. Etching is not a stain. The marble surface actually becomes damaged when an acid comes in contact with marble. To remove an etch from marble, refinishing and re-polishing are required. Etching is a common problem with marble, especially marble countertops. Subsequent chapters will describe how to protect marble from etching. Etching is commonly confused with staining, but it cannot be removed by stain removal techniques or chemicals.

Water Spots

Another common problem associated with staining is the deposit of water spots and water rings. These are the rings left behind from a glass. These rings appear on marble tables and countertops almost everywhere and are caused by slightly acidic liquids running down the sides of the glass and etching the marble. They can also be caused by chemicals in the liquid that deposit minerals on the stone. These are sometimes referred to as *hard water spots*. If the liquid contains calcium or other minerals, it will leave a spot on the marble surface in the shape of the glass bottom. These mineral deposits are the same type that appear in an automatic dishwasher or a glass shower door. These rings and spots usually are not stains and cannot be removed with stain-removing chemicals and poultices. Again, refinishing and re-polishing will probably be necessary.

Efflorescence

Efflorescence is another condition found on stone that is not considered a stain. Efflorescence appears as a white powdery dust on top of stone. If you wipe your hand across the surface of the stone you pick up a light powdery residue. Efflorescence is simply a deposit of minerals on the surface of the stone. These minerals usually come from the setting bed or from the stone itself. When the stone becomes wet during installation or afterward, the water dissolves some of the minerals in the setting bed or stone and carries them to the surface. When the water evaporates, the minerals are left behind in the form of a powder. Subsequent chapters will describe how to avoid and eliminate efflorescence.

Stuns

Stun marks appear on certain marbles as white marks but cannot be felt if you run your finger across the mark. They seem as though they are below the surface. These stun marks are usually caused by an impact on the surface of the stone such as someone dropping a heavy object or a woman walking across the floor with high heels. These marks occur from an explosion of the crystals in certain marbles. This is very similar to glass when it shatters. These marks can be very deep, extending all the way through the marble. They are very difficult to remove, but again, they are not considered stains.

Wet Stone

When most stones become wet, they have a tendency to darken, Figure 1-1. This is especially true when newly installed. The setting bed usually is very wet. The water migrates through the stone to escape and evaporate. This drying process can take a very long time, depending on the temperature, humidity, and airflow. Certain granites can take months to dry. However, you must be sure that you are dealing with a stain and not moisture. Moisture can appear uniform throughout the entire stone, or it can appear blotchy. The best way to determine if you are dealing with wet stone is to purchase a moisture meter. These meters are inexpensive (about $250) and can help detect many problems related to moisture. To avoid buying a moisture meter, take a heat gun or hair dryer to the suspected wet area and see if the area lightens. *Caution: Do not apply too much heat, especially to granite, because it may cause the crystals in the stone to expand and spall or the stone to crack.*

These are just a few stone conditions that are not stains. Before applying any kind of stain remover or chemical you must be sure you are dealing with a stain.

It is also possible to run into combinations of conditions, such as a stain and an etch. Wine is an example of this condition. The tannin in wine will stain the stone, and the acid will etch it. In this case, it is necessary to first remove the stain and then refinish or re-polish the etch.

Figure 1-1. A marble floor several months after a flood. Notice the large dark area. This is moisture that will eventually dry.

STAIN INVESTIGATION

How can you tell if you are dealing with a stain, an etch, or something else? This is difficult unless you are very familiar with all of these conditions. It may be necessary to become a detective. Of course, if you were the one who spilled something on the stone, you will know what it is. If you are a contractor and are called in to look at a stain, you are usually not so lucky as to know what caused the stain. The following paragraphs comprise my investigative process for determining what caused the stain, if in fact it is a stain.

Ask the Customer

Do not play the "know-it-all expert." Ask what the stain is. Chances are the customer who called you to remove the stain knows what was spilled there. Knowing the identity of the stain is half the battle. Once the stain is identified, a proper chemical can be chosen to remove it.

Detective Work

What if the stain is unknown? This is when you need to become a detective and start your own investigation. Why is this so important? Why not apply several different chemicals or poultices and choose which one works? This makes sense except for one problem. Certain stains will become permanently set into the stone with certain chemicals. Iron oxidizes when exposed to bleach and acids. If clay poultices are mixed with acids, the stone may turn brown or yellow. This is caused by the iron in these clays becoming oxidized by the acids. Therefore, it is extremely important to identify the stain as well as you can before applying a poultice.

The Investigation

The next step is to determine if it is a stain. If an acidic material is placed on marble stone, it is going to etch. Etching can range from mild to harsh. If the spot is dull, clouded, or whitish, it may be an etch. Feel the spot. If it is not as smooth as the surrounding surface, you can be sure it is etched. This is not to say that if it is smooth it is not etched. A mild etch will still feel smooth. The simplest way to determine if a marble surface is mildly etched is to place some polishing powder on the etch. Then take a white pad with a little bit of water and work the powder into a creamy slurry, rubbing the slurry across the spot for several minutes. If it is an etch, this process is likely to remove or improve it. If the etch is deep, this simple technique will not work very well. You will need to re-hone the area before you can polish it. You must determine that you're dealing with a stain and not an etch, a wet stone, or a stun mark.

To further investigate, take a look around. Where is the stain? Is it near the stove or refrigerator? This is a good indication that it may have been caused by food or cooking oils. Is there a certain pattern to the stain? Does it appear as a splash? This would indicate that a liquid was dropped.

Does it appear smudged? This would indicate something more solid was dropped. What color is the stain? If it's red and near the refrigerator, it could be ketchup, fruit drink, strawberries, etc. Use some common sense, and try to determine how the stain may have ended up where it is.

It cannot be emphasized enough how important it is to know what caused the stain. If the stain is unknown and you apply chemicals at random, you take the chance of permanently setting the stain.

STAIN TYPES

Stains can generally be classified into two types: *organic* and *inorganic*. Organic stains are caused by those materials that are derived from living organisms. For example, most foods, drinks, plants, and some dyes are considered organic stains. Inorganic stains are those materials that are not derived from living organisms. They are usually mineral in nature; for example, copper and rust.

Why is the distinction between these stain types so important? Inorganic stains are mineral in nature, as are natural stones. Iron is a compound found naturally in stone, and it will oxidize, rust, and cause the stone to turn yellow, brown, or red, Figure 1-2. This occurs quite frequently in white marble and some varieties of limestone. If the stains in these stones are caused by oxidization of iron as part of the stone, then the stains will not come out. This is not to say that organic stains are any easier to remove; but in this case, you will know from the very start if the stain is worth trying to remove.

Determining that the stain is inorganic and caused by natural minerals in the stone can be difficult, but there are a few guidelines that can help. First, if the stain has the same color and is spread entirely over the stone, chances are it may be caused by external staining materials such as old wax, crystallization fluids, iron in the cleaning water, etc. Does the stain follow a certain pattern? Many times

Figure 1-2. Iron staining on white marble exterior

rust will appear in stone and follow a given pattern. For example, in statuary white marble, iron will be noticed adjacent to veining, usually running alongside the length of the vein. If this is the case, it is a good indication that the iron is part of the stone and cannot be removed. If the problem is severe and further analysis is needed, then remove a section of stone. Carefully examine the section of stone, and determine if the staining is on the surface only or through the entire stone. If the stain is all the way through the stone, then it will be difficult or impossible to remove. Examine the setting bed where you removed the section of stone. If it is stained, remove a portion of the setting bed to see how deep the stain is or to determine if the stain is coming from something within the setting bed. Quite often, stray nails or screws will cause iron staining, Figure 1-3. Refer to the troubleshooting guide in Chapter 6 for help on how to remove rust stains.

Organic stains can be difficult to remove depending on their type. For example, when oil is absorbed into a stone, it can quickly spread throughout the stone, even though on the surface, it looks relatively small. To illustrate this point,

Figure 1-3. Iron staining on shower wall due to metal screws

place several drops of oil on a light-colored marble. Wait several days, then turn the stone over, and you will see how the oil spreads itself over the entire stone. This is important to realize when it comes time to remove the oil stain. Of course, the quicker you can treat a stain, the less chance it will have to soak into the stone.

WHAT IS A POULTICE?

A *poultice* is an absorbent material applied to a surface to draw out a stain. It can be a powder, paper, or gel. The most common poultices in use today are powders. A number of powders are very absorbent and are ideal for stain removal. The following are some typical powders used in poultices:

- Clays (atteapulgite, kaolin, fullers earth)
- Talc
- Chalk (whiting)
- Sepiolite (hydrous magnesium silicate)

11

- Diatomaceous earth
- Methyl cellulose

Clays and diatomaceous earth are usually the best. Do not use whiting or clays containing iron. When using acidic chemicals, the acids will react with the iron and may cause yellowing of the stone surface. It is best to purchase poultice powder materials from a reputable supplier of products for stone maintenance.

Some typical paper poultices are cotton balls, paper towels, and gauze pads. Paper poultices can be quite effective on mild stains. They are easier to apply than powder poultices and are also easier to remove.

Gel poultices are usually thick chemical gels that are designed to be applied to a stain without the use of powders or papers. They work effectively with certain stains.

When purchasing poultice materials, ask if they contain stain-removing chemicals or if they need chemicals added. Some powder and gel poultices contain chemicals, and all you need to do is add water. Never mix additional chemicals with a poultice that contains its own chemical formulation.

As stated previously, the reason stone stains is because it is absorbent. In order to remove the stain, this process must be reversed, and the stain must be sucked out of the stone. The poultice is the material necessary to do this. However, once the stain penetrates and becomes attached to the stone, it is very difficult to suck the stain out. Therefore, something must be used to loosen the stain. This loosening is accomplished by matching a chemical to the type of stain. Again, this is why it is important to identify the stain.

STAIN REMOVAL

The removal of stains from stone surfaces can be a difficult task. The following procedure, if followed properly, will make the job much easier (see photo essay at the end of the chapter for correct poultice application procedure).

Step 1. Identify the stain
Knowing what type of stain you are trying to remove is half the battle in stain removal. Ask questions and investigate.

Step 2. Clean the stained area
Just because the stain looks like it is deep in the stone doesn't mean that it cannot be cleaned with stone cleaner. Clean the area thoroughly using a good stone cleaner with a neutral pH. A good, heavy duty stone cleaner may also be used, but first try cleaning with a mild, neutral cleaner. When attempting to remove any stain on stone, always use the most gentle method first, then proceed to more aggressive chemicals and techniques. Cleaning will also remove any surface residue caused by the staining material allowing for faster removal if a poultice is later needed.

Step 3. Remove coatings
If the stone has been coated with wax, acrylics, urethane, or any other topical treatments, it is important to strip the coating before attempting to remove the stain. Most coatings will interfere with the chemicals used to remove stains.

Step 4. Pre-wet
Wet the stained area with distilled water to fill the pores of the stone with water. This isolates the stained area and allows the chemicals that will be used to stay in contact longer with the stain. Pre-wetting will also prevent the chemicals from drying too fast.

Step 5. Prepare the poultice
If a powder poultice is to be used, mix the powder with the chemical you choose (see Chapter 6). Mix the powder and chemical into a thick paste (consistency of creamy peanut butter). You want the mixture to be wet but not so wet that it runs.

If a paper poultice is used, soak the paper in the chemical of choice before applying it to the stain. If a gel poultice is used, apply the gel directly on the stain.

Step 6. Apply the poultice
Carefully apply the poultice to the stained area, overlapping the poultice several inches over the stain. This overlapping is important since the stain may be spread further into the stone than it appears. The thicker the poultice is applied, the longer it will take to dry. Generally, about ¼-in. thick is sufficient for most stains.

Step 7. Cover the poultice
Cover the poultice with plastic, and tape the edges down. Plastic food wrap works great. Be careful to use a tape that will not stain the stone. A low-contact masking tape works well.

Covering the poultice with plastic prevents it from drying out too quickly. It is necessary to keep the poultice wet as long as possible to allow the chemical to work on the stain and loosen it from the stone.

Step 8. Remove the plastic cover
After approximately 24 hours, remove the plastic from the poultice. If the poultice is not yet dry, leave the poultice uncovered until it is dry. This is extremely important. Remember, a poultice works by drawing the stain out of the stone. The drying process is what causes this pulling action.

Step 9. Remove the poultice
After the poultice is thoroughly dry, scrape it off with a razor blade or putty knife. Be careful not to scratch the surface of the stone. Clean any residue of poultice from the stain with water and a neutral cleaner.

Step 10. Examine the stained area
Carefully examine the stained area. If the stain is not

removed, reapply the poultice. It may take several poultices to remove difficult stains. If after two applications of poultice you do not see any lightening of the stain, then your chemical choice may be incorrect or the stain may not be removable.

The removal of stains is not an exact science. Some stains may be permanent and will almost never come out. Be careful not to waste too much time applying poultices. If the type of stone is still available and you can obtain a close match, it may be easier and cheaper to replace the stone.

POULTICE APPLICATION PROCEDURE

The following is a photo essay illustrating the steps for correct poultice application as outlined above:

Step 1. Identify the stain — In this example, wine stain on travertine

Steps 2 and 3. Clean the stained area and remove any coatings

Step 4. Pre-wet the stained area

Step 5. Prepare and mix the poultice

Step 6. Apply the poultice

Step 7. Cover the poultice

Step 8. Wait 24 hours, then remove the cover

Step 9. Remove the poultice

Step 10. Examine the stained area and repeat steps 2-9 until stain is gone

CHAPTER 2

STAIN CHEMISTRY

How often in your attempt to remove a stain have you grabbed the first cleaner you could get your hands on and haphazardly poured it on the stain? It didn't work, so you grabbed something else and tried it. That didn't work either. By the time you were done trying all the chemicals you could get your hands on, you had a bigger mess than what you started with. What happened? With a little knowledge of chemical properties, you can put an end to the guesswork associated with this problem.

A basic knowledge of chemistry is extremely important when dealing with stain removal. Mixing the wrong chemicals can cause some serious damage to the stone surface as well as to yourself. Everyone should know that you do not mix bleach and ammonia together, because they will form a fatal gas. The chemicals dealt with in stain removal are as dangerous as these two common grocery store chemicals.

CHEMICALS AND CHEMISTRY

Chemistry is the science of chemical properties, compositions, reactions, and the uses of a substance. For example, when you pour an acidic chemical on a piece of marble, the acid attacks the calcium in the marble. This is a chemical reaction. When you mix a detergent in water you are creating a solution that has different properties than the individual chemicals (the water and the detergent). Chemistry is the study of these changes. Knowing how these individual chemicals react with one another and with the stone you apply them to is important in determining which chemical to use.

What happens when acid is poured on marble? Marble is made of a compound called *calcium carbonate*, which is represented by the chemical formula $CaCO_3$. An acid can also be represented by its chemical formula depending on the type of acid. For example, hydrochloric acid is HCl. When poured on stone, this acid bubbles and fizzes and produces a dull etch mark. What happened? The calcium carbonate ($CaCO_3$) was destroyed by the acid (HCl). This is represented by the following equation:

$$CaCO_3 + HCl \rightarrow Ca + Cl + H_2O + CO_2$$

The acid (HCl) broke the bond between the calcium and the carbonate and produced calcium chloride (CaCl), water (H_2O), and carbon dioxide (CO_2). The fizzing smoke was the carbon dioxide gas escaping into the air.

Listed below are some common acids and their chemical formulas:

Hydrochloric acid (muriatic acid)	HCl
Oxalic acid (polishing compounds)	$H_2C_2O_4$
Acetic acid (vinegar)	CH_3COOH
Sulfamic acid (grout cleaners)	SO_3NH_3
Sulfuric acid (batteries)	H_2SO_4
Phosphoric acid (bathroom cleaners)	H_3PO_4
Hydrofluoric acid (rust removers)	HF

All acids have different strengths; some are weak and some are very strong. The pH scale is used to measure their strength.

WHAT IS pH?

What is pH, and how does it apply to stain removal? pH is used to express the acidity or alkalinity of a chemical liquid. pH only applies to water-based chemicals. Solvents like mineral spirits, toluene, acetone, etc., do not have a pH.

The measurement of how acidic or alkaline a solution is can be determined by measurement with litmus paper or a pH meter. Both litmus paper and pH meters are available at scientific supply or marble supply dealers. The readings obtained are compared to the pH scale.

pH Scale

The pH scale ranges from 1 to 14, Figure 2-1. A substance with a pH of 1 or more but less than 7 is considered an acid. A pH above 7, 8 to 14, is considered an alkaline. A pH of 7 is neutral, neither acid nor alkaline. We are often told in the stone industry to "use a neutral cleaner on your stone." This is referring to a cleaner with a pH of 7, or neutral.

The pH strength is determined by where on the pH scale the solution falls. On the acidic side of the pH scale, the lower the number the stronger the acid. Therefore, a pH of 3 is stronger than a pH of 4. On the alkaline side, the higher the number the stronger the alkalinity. Therefore, a pH of 10 is stronger than a pH of 9. For each whole step up or down on the pH scale, the strength increases or decreases by 10 times. For example, a pH of 3 is ten times stronger than a pH of 4 and 100 times stronger than a pH of 5 and so forth. A pH of 11 is ten times stronger than a pH of 10 and 100 times stronger than a pH of 9 and so on.

1	2	3	4	5	6	[7]	8	9	10	11	12	13	14

(1 to 6 — acid)   (7 — neutral)   (8 to 14 — alkaline)

Figure 2-1. pH scale

What does all this mean in relation to maintaining stone surfaces? Calcium-based stones such as marble are very reactive with acids. If an acid such as lemon or vinegar is placed on a polished stone, it will etch the surface and leave a dull spot. Common sense tells us to keep acids away from polished marble. On the other hand, granite contains no acid-sensitive minerals, and acids generally will not affect granites. One acid of exception here is hydrofluoric acid, which is strong enough to etch granites.

What about alkaline chemicals? Alkaline chemicals are found in heavy duty stone cleaners, floor strippers, ammonia, sodium hydroxide (lye), etc. For the most part, alkaline chemicals are safe to use on most stone surfaces. However, alkalines can cause some problems if you're not careful. When using alkalines be sure to thoroughly rinse the surface to remove all alkaline solution. Alkalines can leave a residue on the surface of the stone, so rinsing is crucial. If alkaline cleaners are allowed to sit too long on the surface of a stone, the solution will penetrate into the pores of the stone, dry out, and possibly cause the stone to spall. This spalling is caused by the formation of salts when the alkaline solution dries. Some agglomerate stones are sensitive to alkaline cleaners. Agglomerates contain polyester binders that hold the stone together, which can be attacked by certain alkaline solutions. When in doubt, always test first.

WATER- AND SOLVENT-BASED CHEMICALS

All of the chemicals dealt with in stain removal can be classified into two general categories: *water-based* or *solvent-based*. Water-based chemicals are those chemicals containing water. All the ingredients that are mixed with the water are soluble in water. Some examples of water-based chemicals are stone soaps, liquid dishwashing soaps, bleach, ammonia, and acrylic coatings, Table 2-1. Solvent-based chemicals are waterless chemicals. The ingredients mixed in the solution are soluble in other solvents such as alcohols and hydrocarbons. Some examples of solvent-based chemicals are silicone impregnators, paraffin waxes, mineral spirits, acetone, methylene chloride, polyurethane, epoxies, and polyesters, Table 2-2. There are hundreds of different solvents, and Table 2-2 is only a partial list of the most commonly used solvents.

Chemical	Common Name	Found In
Acids	Acid	Polishing powders, stone cleaners, toilet bowl and bathroom cleaners, grout cleaners, rust removers
Ammonia	Ammonia	Wax strippers, floor cleaners, acrylic coatings
Hydrogen peroxide	Wood bleach	Hair color developer, bleaching agents, laundry detergents
Bleach	Bleach	Household bleach, laundry detergents
Surfactant	Soaps	Stone soaps, dishwashing soap, etc.
Tri-sodium phosphate	TSP	Floor cleaners, general purpose cleaners
Sodium hydroxide	Lye	Laundry detergents, wax strippers, stone cleaners

Table 2-1. Examples of water-based chemicals

Solvent	Common Name	Found In
Mineral spirits	Paint thinner	Impregnators, cleaners
Acetone	Acetone	Fingernail polish remover
Alcohols	Alcohol	Impregnators, strippers
d-limonene	Terpene	Cleaners
Naphtha	Naphtha	Paint strippers, impregnators
Xylene	Xylene	Paint strippers
Trichloroethane	1-1-1 tri	Paint strippers, impregnators
Methylene chloride	Methyl chloride	Paint strippers, furniture strippers
Toluene	Toluene	Paint strippers, impregnators
Methyl ethyl ketone	MEK	Paint cleaners and strippers
Benzene	Benzene	Paint cleaners and strippers

Table 2-2. Examples of solvent-based chemicals

Knowing which chemical will work on certain stains is important. If the stain, coating, or whatever is being removed is water based, then a water-based chemical will most likely be needed to remove it. On the other hand, if the stain or coating is solvent based, then a solvent will be needed to remove it. Of course there are exceptions to this rule, but generally this will help in choosing the proper chemical. For example, when trying to remove a coating of polyurethane from a stone surface, we know that most polyurethanes are solvent-based and therefore will most likely require a solvent to remove them. Polyurethane is not soluble in water, and most water-based chemicals will not remove it. *Caution: There are now new water-based polyurethanes and water-based strippers that will remove these types of coatings. These strippers are new and generally require a very long dwell time, but they are safer than solvent-based chemicals.*

How do you determine if a chemical is water-based or solvent-based? This is relatively easy. First, obtain a Material Safety Data Sheet, commonly called an M.S.D.S. The M.S.D.S. provides safety information that may be needed in case of a spill, fire, or medical emergency. On the M.S.D.S. there will be a section that lists a material's flash point. Most solvents have a flash point. Water does not have a flash point. If the chemical has no flash point, chances are it is water-based. Another good indicator is the boiling point. The boiling point of water is 212°F. If the boiling point of the chemical is 212°F, it may be a water-based chemical. But be careful, because some solvents also have boiling points of 212°F. The simplest way to determine if a chemical is solvent- or water-based is to become familiar with the basic solvents (refer to Table 2-2).

CHAPTER 3

STAIN PROTECTION

How do you protect stone and other porous materials from staining? There are so many sealers on the market today, but which ones are the best and which ones really work? It can be very confusing trying to choose a sealer to protect stone. In the past several years, the stone restoration and janitorial industries have bombarded the market with hundreds of products to seal, protect, and polish stone. Fortunately, all of these products fall into only two major categories: *coatings* and *impregnators* or *penetrating sealers*.

COATINGS

Coatings are sealers that place a sacrificial coating on the surface of the stone. This is a film that lays on top of the stone, acting as a barrier to prevent water, oil, and dirt from entering the pores of the stone. Coatings can be classified into two general types: *strippable* and *permanent*.

Strippable Coatings

Strippable coatings are coatings that are designed to be easily stripped or removed from the surface of the stone. These coatings are made of polymers consisting of acrylics, styrene, polyethylene, and others. They are usually water based. Many of the janitorial products are water-based, polymer-type coatings. To identify these coatings, look for terms on the label such as "metal cross link," "high solids," "high speed," "acrylic," "thermoplastic," etc. When in doubt, ask. There are hundreds of different formulas of strippable floor coatings. Most of them are designed for resilient tile floors and not for stone. If a coating is to be used, be sure it is specified for stone.

Permanent Coatings

Permanent coatings are coatings that are very difficult to remove. They are made of solvent-based polymers such as polyurethane, epoxies, etc. These are not recommended for stone.

IMPREGNATORS OR PENETRATING SEALERS

Some impregnators are designed to penetrate below the surface of a stone and deposit solid particles in the pores. Others are designed to coat the individual minerals below the surface of the stone. Water, oil, and dirt are restricted from entering the stone. Impregnators can be solvent- or water-based and usually contain silicone, siloxane, silane, methyl silicate, or other similar silicone derivatives. Impregnators can also be classified into two types: hydrophobic (water repelling) and oleophobic (oil repelling).

Hydrophobic Impregnators

Hydrophobic impregnators are designed to repel only water and water-based chemicals. Fruit drinks, coffee, tea, soda, etc., would be repelled by a hydrophobic impregnator.

Oleophobic Impregnators

Oleophobic impregnators are designed to repel water- and oil-based liquids. Cooking oil, grease, body oils, etc., would be repelled by an oleophobic impregnator.

An oleophobic impregnator will always be hydrophobic, but a hydrophobic impregnator may not be oleophobic. Be sure to read product labels carefully to determine if they are hydrophobic or oleophobic. Some products are listed as oil resistant. Oil resistant and oil repellent are entirely different. Oil resistant will only slow down the absorption of oil into the stone. Oil repellent will prevent oil from entering the stone. Again, read product labels carefully. Be sure you are buying the right product for your particular situation. *Caution: Do not choose an impregnator to protect the stone from acid etching. Impregnators do not make the stone acid resistant.*

CHOOSING THE PROPER SEALER

Many factors need to be considered when choosing the correct sealer, such as stone type, stone finish, stone location, and current maintenance. These four factors are described in further detail below.

Stone Type

All stone is not created equal. How porous a stone is and how fast it will absorb a liquid is called the *absorption coefficient*. This coefficient is extremely important when choosing a sealer. Granite generally will have a higher absorption coefficient than a polished marble. Limestone can be extremely absorbent. The higher the absorption coefficient, the more difficult it will be to seal the stone.

For a general idea of how absorbent the stone is, place several drops of water on the surface of the stone and time how long it takes for the water to completely disappear. If the water disappears in under one minute, consider the stone very porous. If it takes up to three or four minutes, consider it porous. If it takes more than four minutes, consider the stone slightly porous. This simple test will also give a good indication of the quantity of sealer needed to protect the entire area.

Stone Finish

The finish on a stone affects its absorption coefficient. A polished surface will be less absorbent than a honed or flamed finish. The absorption test just described will determine how absorbent a stone is. Table 3-1 describes the various finishes available on stone surfaces.

Finish Type	Description
Polished	A highly reflective finish
Honed	A smooth finish with little to no reflectivity; usually with a maximum of a 400# hone
Flamed or thermal	A finish achieved by passing a flame across the surface of the stone causing the stone to spall and resulting in a rough, uneven surface
Tooled or bushhammered	A finish achieved by hammering the surface of the stone with a chiseled tool
Sawcut	The finish that remains on a stone after it has been cut; easily identified by the circular pattern left from the saw
Sandblasted	A rough finish achieved by abrading the surface of the stone with high pressure sand

Table 3-1. Listing of various stone finishes

Stone Location

Where is the stone located? Is the stone on the floor, wall, or countertop? Is it in a kitchen, foyer, lobby, or bathroom? What type of abuse is it exposed to? Water, oil, heavy traffic, pets, etc., all need to be taken into consideration when choosing the proper product for protection. For example, a marble kitchen floor that is used daily will need a sealer that has oleophobic properties. At the other extreme, a front foyer that will only be exposed to the occasional tracking of wet feet would only require a hydrophobic sealer. When protecting a busy hotel lobby floor, a wax coating may track and scuff too easily. In this case, an impregnator and a polishing program may be needed to maintain the shine.

Current Maintenance

How is the stone maintained? If a marble floor is mopped daily, it may be exposed to harsh cleaning chemicals. If maintenance is neglected, a stone floor will have ground-in dirt and grit, and if it has a high polish it will be worn. In this case, no matter how well it is protected, it will become dirty and dull. For example, a moderately busy hotel lobby floor that is dust mopped and wet mopped every day may only need a light coating of marble wax or finish. On the other hand, a stone foyer floor located in a home that does not receive much traffic does not need daily cleaning. An application of a hydrophobic impregnator may be all that is necessary.

The type of stone, its finish, its location, and how it is maintained all need to be considered when determining how to protect it. Evaluate each of these parameters carefully.

COATING OR IMPREGNATOR?

How do you make the determination between a coating or an impregnator? They both have their advantages and their disadvantages. The following summary should be studied carefully when choosing the proper product:

Coatings — Advantages

As stated previously, coatings are sealers that place a protective, sacrificial layer on the surface of the stone. The following is a list of some of the advantages of using coatings:

- They are generally economical, and the cost of the initial application is relatively low.
- They are generally easy to apply, and unskilled labor can learn to apply them in a short time.
- They generally provide a sacrificial coating on the stone, which will take most of the wear, preventing wear on the stone.
- Certain coatings provide added slip-resistance.
- They can be applied below grade. If a floor is located below ground level, a good coating may prove beneficial for protecting or waterproofing.
- They generally provide various degrees of luster.

Coatings — Disadvantages

- Since most coatings are typically softer than the stone itself, they will usually scratch, mar, and scuff very easily, showing traffic patterns soon after application. This will require frequent buffing, burnishing, or re-application.
- Coatings can build up and cause an unsightly appearance, producing an unnatural, wavy, plastic look to the stone.

+ Poor quality coatings can turn yellow, especially if the stone is exposed to UV light.
+ Coatings require frequent stripping and reapplication. The chemicals and abrasives used in the stripping process may cause damage to the stone. Typically, certain stripping pads and stripping brushes can scratch some softer stones. Some wax strippers can harm certain stones such as agglomerates, eating away at the polyester binders.
+ Certain coatings may block the breathing capability of the stone. Moisture can become trapped below the surface and lead to spalling.

Impregnators — Advantages
+ Most impregnators do not change the appearance of the stone.
+ Most impregnators do not require frequent applications. Since the impregnator is below the surface, it will generally last several years before reapplication is necessary.
+ Most impregnators are not affected by UV light since they are below the surface where UV light cannot penetrate. For this reason, they can be used outdoors.
+ Impregnators are typically hydrophobic, while some are oleophobic.

Impregnators — Disadvantages
+ Impregnators that are solvent based produce noxious and flammable vapors during application.
+ Solvent-based impregnators are harmful to the environment producing high VOCs (volatile organic compounds). For this reason, some are restricted in certain states. Always check the M.S.D.S. sheet.
+ Impregnators require a semi-skilled person for application. Proper training is highly recommended.
+ The initial cost of most impregnators is relatively high.

- Impregnators in general cannot be used below grade to resist hydrostatic pressure. Since the stone is still capable of breathing, water can be forced through the stone by pressure.

These guidelines should help when choosing the proper product for protection. Always talk with the manufacturer or distributor, and let them know where you plan to use their product. They can be very helpful if you tell them all the conditions that apply.

CHAPTER 4

QUESTIONS AND ANSWERS

STAINS

Question

We have Italian marble on the lobby floors in our commercial office buildings. Recently we noticed several problems: 1) entire tiles are evenly discoloring yellow or gray; and 2) rust-like stains are appearing in an area near the door. What is causing these problems? What should we do to correct the problems and prevent any further damage?

Answer

The yellowing and graying of certain Italian and Greek white marbles is a common problem. There are several possible causes for this condition:

1. Maintenance techniques: Take a close look at your maintenance program. Are you using certain waxes or acrylics that may be causing this yellowing? There are several products on the market that are not designed for use on marble and may turn yellow over time.

2. Iron minerals: Certain white marbles will begin to yellow, turn gray, or darken naturally over time. The cause for this condition usually is the result of iron minerals in the marble itself. Some white marbles contain rather high

37

concentrations of ferrous oxide (iron). When the stone is set, these iron deposits do not appear until several months or sometimes several years after installation. In these cases, the iron is slowly oxidizing, triggered by moisture from daily cleaning, the setting bed, or simply by humid conditions. This is similar to a shiny piece of metal that rusts when exposed to air and water.

3. Other sources: The rust staining near the entry door can be caused by the previous two reasons but most likely is coming from a number of other sources. Check to see if there is any metal nearby. For example, thresholds attached with metal screws may cause this staining when the screws rust. If the building is located in a northern climate, de-icing compounds, some of which contain iron, may be the cause. Are walk-off mats being used? Walk-off mats can hold moisture under them and will cause rusting if this moisture contains any iron. Clean under these mats frequently.

Solution to Cause #1

If these coatings are causing the yellowing or graying, a strong alkaline wax stripper will correct the problem. Be careful not to use an abrasive that may scratch the marble. There are several strippers on the market that will remove these coatings with very little agitation.

Also, check the type of cleaner you are using. Make sure it is a neutral pH cleaner and that it is designed for use on marble and other types of stone. Make sure the mop that is being used is clean and rinsed frequently. A dirty mop and dirty mop water will also cause a white stone to take on a gray or yellow appearance very quickly.

Graying of certain white marbles is also common when certain polishing methods are used that require steel wool for buffing. If steel wool is being used, make absolutely sure that the floor is dry. If the steel wool is being used while the floor contains any moisture, it will certainly gray, and the steel wool will oxidize and yellow.

Solution to Cause #2

Unfortunately, once this condition exists it is very difficult, if not impossible, to correct. Several chemicals have been used successfully to improve this condition. Mildly acidic rust removers can work effectively to remove the yellowing. Be careful, because these rust removers will etch the marble, and re-honing and polishing will have to be done after treating with these products. Always test a small area first to determine if these chemicals will provide the desired results. Other chemicals used effectively on iron staining are sodium hydrosulfite and sodium metabisulfite. These chemicals work well both in a poultice and alone as a remover. Be sure to follow package directions carefully, and always test first.

Yellowing can also be caused by minerals with iron in the setting bed. If the initial setting was done using a mortar or water that was high in iron, the iron may be leaching through the marble and causing the staining. If the problem is severe enough, remove a tile and send both the tile and a sample of the setting material to a testing lab for analysis. This test is inexpensive and could provide an answer to where the yellowing is coming from.

Solution to Cause #3

Apply several test poultices to stained areas to remove the rust. There are several available from your marble supplier.

There are as many solutions as there are causes for marble to gray and yellow. If an answer cannot be found, contact a professional restoration company to evaluate the problem.

Question

I have been poulticing a stain on a red granite countertop using a clay poultice and a commercial degreaser. When I remove the poultice, the area where the poultice was is very dark and does not seem to dry out and lighten. What causes this, and how can I bring the granite back to its original color?

Answer

This is a very common problem on granite. Granite is more porous than most marbles. Because of its porous nature, granite has the ability to retain a great deal of moisture. The dark area in this case may simply be excessive moisture. Some moisture spots take a week or more to dry out; however, there is a trick to accelerate the drying process. The simplest way to draw out this moisture is to apply a dry poultice. Place a large quantity of dry poultice (without any added chemicals or water) over the dark area, overlapping about ½ in. Allow this poultice to remain on the dark area for approximately 12 hours. If the area is still dark, allow the dry poultice to sit longer. If the poultice becomes wet or damp, remove it and apply a new dry poultice.

If after 24 hours the dark area has not become lighter, then there are several other possible causes. The degreaser may have contributed to the darkening. If this is the case, reapply a plain poultice with only a water additive. This should dilute the degreaser and pull any excess degreaser out. There is also the possibility that the original stain was deeply embedded, and the poultice only pulled it closer to the surface. Repeat the poulticing several times to completely remove the stain.

Question

If I seal a stone with an impregnator and the stone becomes stained, will a poultice work?

Answer

Yes, a poultice should work as long as the stain occurred after the stone was sealed. If the stain was present before the sealer was applied, there is a good chance the stain will be sealed into the stone making removal difficult. In this case, the sealer will have to be removed by first using a strong solvent such as methylene chloride, then applying a poultice to remove the stain.

Question
How long should I continue to poultice a stain?

Answer
There is no rule for the number of times a stain needs to be poulticed. Generally, if the stain is slowly disappearing, continue poulticing. The average number of poultice applications will be about five.

Question
Can I re-use poultice powder?

Answer
The re-use of poultice powder is not recommended. Chemicals tend to lose their strength and may not store very well. It is always best to apply fresh poultice.

Question
How important is it for a poultice to dry thoroughly?

Answer
It is very important. If the poultice is removed while it is still wet, it may not draw the stain from the stone. The drying action is what causes the stain to be removed.

Question
Can I mix several different chemicals together in the same poultice? For example, can I use an acid and hydrogen peroxide together?

Answer
Absolutely not! Never mix chemicals together unless you are instructed to on the product's instructions. Mixing certain chemicals can be dangerous to you as well as the stone.

Question

I have heard that using distilled water in a poultice is better than tap water. Is this true?

Answer

Yes, use distilled water whenever it is available. Tap water can sometimes contain minerals such as chlorine, iron, and others that can retard stain removal.

Question

I am having trouble applying a poultice to a wall. It keeps running down. How can I get it to stick to the wall?

Answer

The easiest way to apply a poultice to a wall is to use less water or chemical in the poultice. This will keep it from sagging. You should also apply the poultice in a thin layer. Another technique is to apply the poultice to a piece of plastic first, then place the poultice and plastic combination on the wall with the poultice portion facing the wall. Immediately tape the bottom of the plastic and then the remaining sides. It may also help to place a piece of tape along the bottom of the plastic prior to placing it on the wall.

Question

When I remove a poultice there seems to be a ring or halo around the stained area. How do I remove it?

Answer

The halo or ring usually is caused by a residue of poultice. Try cleaning the halo area with the chemical you used in the poultice, and be sure to rinse it with plenty of water. If this does not remove the halo or ring, it is possible that the surrounding area is dirty and the poultice has cleaned the stained area. In this case, clean the entire area with a good heavy duty cleaner.

Question
I have a very large wall to poultice, several thousand square feet. How can I apply the poultice to this large area?

Answer
If you use a poultice that is fine enough, it can be sprayed on with a texture gun. Texture guns can be purchased at supply houses that specialize in stucco spraying. Mix a large quantity of poultice in a 5-gallon bucket using a slow rpm drill and mixing paddle. Pour the mixture into the spray gun hopper and spray.

Question
Can I speed up the drying time of a poultice?

Answer
Yes, but only if the poultice has stayed wet for at least 12 hours. If the drying time is too rapid there may not be adequate time for the chemicals to react. Drying time can be accelerated by placing fans near the poultice.

Question
Can a poultice be used on other surfaces besides stone?

Answer
Yes, most poultice powders can be used on any porous surface such as concrete, Mexican tile, ceramic tile, porcelain tile, cultured marble, Corian™, etc. However, always be sure to test first for compatibility.

Question
Once I remove a stain, what are the chances of it coming back?

Answer
It may come back depending on how deep the stain is or what caused the stain in the first place. If the stain is coming

from behind the stone, chances are it will come back. If this is the case and the stain reappears, replace the stone whenever possible.

Question
How do I dispose of used poultice? Is it safe to dump down the drain?

Answer
This depends on what chemical was used in the poultice. The M.S.D.S. should describe how to dispose of the chemical.

Question
Can a poultice be used outdoors?

Answer
Yes, but be sure to cover it with plastic in case of rain. The poultice may also dry too rapidly outdoors. In this case, try covering it with black plastic to block the sunlight.

Question
Should I use hot or cold water when mixing a poultice?

Answer
Always use cold to warm water. Certain chemicals will become very reactive in hot water and can be dangerous.

Question
Is it advisable to hone a polished stone before applying a poultice?

Answer
It is not necessary to hone a polished stone prior to applying a poultice, but honing will open the pores of the stone allowing for increased dwell time of the chemical.

Question
What is the ideal temperature for a poultice to be applied?

Answer
There is no ideal temperature; however, a poultice will work best at temperatures above 75°F. Do not apply a poultice in temperatures below freezing.

Question
I have been poulticing a rust stain on a marble floor for several applications. Every time I remove the poultice the stain seems to be darker and more widespread. What is happening?

Answer
Chances are the source of the rust is under the marble. A nail or metal object may have been left behind when the marble was installed. The reason the rust is getting darker is because the poultice is pulling the rust from the bottom of the stone to the top. The best solution is to remove the marble and find the source of the rust.

Question
I just finished having my white Thassos marble floor polished. After two days the entire floor turned yellow. What should I do?

Answer
What process was used to polish the floor? This problem occurs with Thassos marble when a process known as *recrystallization* has been used. If this was the process that was used, the entire floor will have to be honed to remove the yellowing. The yellowing is probably due to a reaction of the chemicals in the recrystallization product and the iron in the marble. Not all recrystallization products cause this yellowing. Always test an area prior to polishing the entire floor.

Question

We recently removed a large carpet from our terrazzo floor. Under the carpet was a large yellowed area the shape of the carpet. How do we remove this yellow stain?

Answer

This is a common problem with carpets that have jute or rubber backings. Moisture becomes trapped under the carpet and causes the dye in the backing to bleed into the terrazzo. To remove the yellowing, clean the area thoroughly with a good detergent, then poultice with a 20% to 50% hydrogen peroxide solution and diatomaceous earth. It may require several poultices to remove the stain. If the carpet remained on the floor for a very long time, the stain may never completely disappear.

Question

We have a large water fountain in our hotel lobby made of coral stone with a copper basin that holds the water. The copper is causing the coral stone to turn green, and there are large green and white deposits trapped in the holes of the stone. We have tried all kinds of chemicals, but nothing seems to remove these deposits. Do you have any suggestions?

Answer

The hard, green deposits are a combination of calcium deposits from the water and copper from the basin. The easiest way to remove them is to use a pressure washer. Be sure to test the pressure washer on an inconspicuous area, since too high a pressure may cause the stone to break apart. Try about 900 psi.

Another method would be to sandblast the deposits from the holes with a micro-blaster — a small sandblaster similar to an airbrush. When you are done removing the large portions of deposits, a mild acid wash should remove the remaining deposits.

Question

I am the facilities manager of an historical church built before the turn of the century. The church is made of a gray granite and has been attacked by vandals with spray paint. How do we remove the paint without destroying the stone?

Answer

There are several methods that can be used to remove spray paint. Since the church is an historical property, it is important to contact a professional who has had experience with historical buildings. Time is of the essence. The quicker you can remove the paint, the less likely it will penetrate deeply into the stone. Until you can contact a professional, try the following cleaning methods:

1. If the stone is polished, try scraping the paint with a very sharp razor blade. If the spray paint dried quickly, chances are it can be removed by scraping.
2. Wash the area with a mild detergent, warm water, and a stiff nylon brush.
3. If either of the two methods above do not remove the graffiti, call a professional who can apply a poultice.

Professionals should try the following after testing first to determine if the cleaning chemicals to be used will damage the stone or cause an undesirable color change:

1. Try cleaning the paint with a solvent such as acetone or mineral spirits.
2. If the stain is deep, a poultice is necessary. Test several poultices using the following solvents:

   ◇ Mineral spirits
   ◇ Toluene
   ◇ Non-methylene chloride paint remover
   ◇ Methylene chloride

The poultice should consist of diatomaceous earth and a solvent. After removing the poultices, be sure the surface has not changed color. Do not perform any testing during the winter months, since cold temperatures can cause the chemicals used to damage the stone.

Question
We have an interior granite wall that has some silicone caulking in the grout joints. The silicone caused staining along the grout edges. We poulticed the stain and successfully removed the staining, but after three months the stain is returning. Why is this happening?

Answer
First, did you remove the silicone caulking? If the source of the stain is not removed it will continue to be a problem. Remove the silicone caulking, and replace it with a non-staining urethane caulking.

If you did remove the silicone caulking and the stain is reappearing, chances are you only removed the silicone from the surface of the stone. Any remaining silicone in the stone has migrated toward the surface. You may need to poultice the stain several times to remove all of the silicone.

Question
We have a stone building (circa 1900) that is in dire need of cleaning. What is the best time of year to schedule cleaning?

Answer
This depends on the climate in which your building is located. If the building is located in the northern hemisphere, never schedule cleaning during the winter months, since freezing temperatures can cause the stone to spall. The best times are in late spring or early fall.

If your building is located in a semi-tropical or tropical climate, never schedule cleaning during the hottest summer months. The heat will cause the cleaning chemicals to evaporate too rapidly. The best time for scheduling cleaning in these areas would be winter, spring, or late fall.

Question
After cleaning a limestone building, the stone turned a brownish-yellow hue that wasn't there prior to cleaning. Why is this occurring?

Answer
This is a common problem with limestone and some marbles. This is usually caused by a high content of iron in the water used to clean the stone. Use a chelating agent in the wash water such as EDTA (ethylene diamine tetra-acetic acid) or an equivalent. A chelating agent will keep the iron suspended in solution so that it doesn't settle on the stone and cause staining.

To remove the yellow hue, try re-washing the stone with water and a chelating agent. If this doesn't work, a re-wash with a commercial rust remover may be necessary.

Question
We have a limestone wall with a heavy growth of moss and lichens all over it. Will this growth deteriorate the stone?

Answer
It may. Lichens and mosses produce oxalic acid, which can destroy calcium-based stones. Since they are considered plants, they will also attract moisture, which can cause all kinds of problems with the stone, including spalling.

SEALERS
Question
Will the application of an impregnator make stone slippery?

Answer

If the product you are using is a true impregnator, it will not add to or subtract from the slip-resistance of the stone. Impregnators are designed to penetrate below the surface of the stone. Check the product label carefully.

Question

If we apply a silicone impregnator to the back of stone before setting, will this cause a bonding problem?

Answer

Yes, it may cause a bonding problem. Since most setting mortars are water based, they will want to repel the water. If this is necessary, use an epoxy-type setting material.

Question

Can an impregnator be overapplied?

Answer

Yes. To properly apply an impregnator, it is important that the stone be thoroughly saturated with sealer. If too much sealer is applied, it will puddle on the surface. This excess should be removed, otherwise it will dry and form a sticky residue. If this happens, simply remove the sealer using mineral spirits. To prevent puddling, remove any excess impregnator with a dry towel.

Question

Does a stone have to be completely dry before applying an impregnator?

Answer

The stone should be completely dry for the sealer to work its best. If the stone is still wet, the sealer will not penetrate areas were water is present; therefore, that portion of the stone will remain unsealed. If the stone has some moisture, the impregnator may have some effect, but the impregnator should be reapplied after the stone has had time to dry.

Question
Is it safe to use an impregnator on a kitchen countertop?

Answer
Yes, it is completely safe. According to a report by the USDA, once the sealer cures it is safe to use in food areas. Wait approximately 24 hours after the application before using the area for food preparation to allow the solvents to evaporate.

Question
Can an impregnator be used to waterproof stone?

Answer
No. The idea of an impregnator is to make the stone water resistant, not waterproof. In order to make the stone waterproof, the stone's pores must be completely blocked. If this is desired, use a topical coating.

Question
Will a silicone impregnator turn a limestone floor dark?

Answer
All silicone-based impregnators should be tested first in an inconspicuous area. Certain limestones and an occasional granite will become permanently dark. Apply the impregnator and wait at least 24 hours before determining if any darkening of the stone will be permanent.

Question

Once a stone is sealed, how much time can pass after something is dropped on the treated stone before it must be cleaned up?

Answer

All sealers, both impregnators and coatings, are designed to slow down the staining process. This does not mean that you can leave the spill on the stone indefinitely. It is always good practice to clean any spills as quickly as possible. *Note: Certain sealers will only slow down the staining process; the stone will still stain if the spill is left long enough.*

Question

Once I seal a stone with a silicone impregnator, how long will it last and when must it be reapplied?

Answer

This will depend on the product. Read the product data sheet carefully. Generally, most silicone impregnators will last several years under normal conditions. If the stone is re-honed or re-polished, reapplication is necessary.

Question

How can I tell if a sealer is no longer working?

Answer

The best way to tell is to perform an absorbency test as follows:

Take a drop or two of water, and place it on the surface of the stone. Record the time it takes to soak into the stone. If the water soaks into the stone in under five minutes, the sealer may no longer be working, reapply.

Question

How do I apply an impregnator to a vertical wall surface?

Answer

The best way to apply an impregnator to a vertical wall is to use a roller, cloth, or lambs wool applicator. Thoroughly saturate the applicator with sealer, and apply it to the wall from the bottom up. Continue to apply the sealer making sure to thoroughly saturate the surface. This may require several applications. Clean any excess sealer off the wall by wiping it with a dry cloth. This will prevent any streaking.

Question

Will a coating adhere to stone that has already been treated with a silicone impregnator?

Answer

Probably not. If the coating is water based, it may have difficulty bonding and may peel off. If a coating is desired, use a coating that has a solvent base.

Question

Is there any way to remove a silicone impregnator from stone?

Answer

There is no effective way to remove 100% of the silicone. Solvents such as mineral spirits, methylene chloride, and others can be used to remove the silicone from the surface to a few millimeters below the surface. These solvents have to be flooded and allowed to sit on the surface for several hours. This can be dangerous, however, and the results may not be acceptable.

Question

If I apply a silicone impregnator to a stone that has a stain on it, can I remove the stain after I seal?

Answer

Chances are you have sealed the stain into the stone permanently. You may be able to remove it using very strong solvents, such as methylene chloride, to remove the sealer rather than attempting a poultice on the stain.

Question

Will I need to apply more of a silicone impregnator to a honed stone than a polished stone?

Answer

A honed surface usually requires more sealer than a polished surface. Honed and textured surfaces are more porous, because the pores of the stone are more open than in a polished stone.

Question

When I attempt to apply an impregnator to a polished stone surface it stays on top and beads. Why is this happening?

Answer

First, check to see if there are any coatings on the surface of the stone. Use a wax stripper, and remove any coatings before applying the sealer. Also check to see if the stone has been sealed before. Perform an absorbency test as outlined earlier in this section.

Question

I have just finished grinding a marble floor. How long do I have to wait before applying a silicone impregnator?

Answer

You need to wait until the stone is completely dry. The average time is about 24 hours depending on temperature and humidity.

Question
Can I speed up the drying time of a silicone impregnator?

Answer
Several fans directed at the stone will help speed the drying and curing time.

Question
After I applied a silicone impregnator, a sticky film developed on the surface. When I walk on the surface I leave footprints. What is wrong?

Answer
You most likely applied too much sealer and did not properly remove the excess. Wipe the floor with mineral spirits, and dry buff the floor with a white pad or cloth.

Question
I applied a water-based penetrating sealer to a marble floor, and it left a very thin film on the surface that has a rainbow color to it. I have tried everything to remove it, and it won't budge. How can I remove this film?

Answer
This is a common problem with water-based impregnators that contain sodium methylsilicanate. The film can only be removed by re-polishing the floor with polishing powder and a buff-colored pad. If the film is very thick, it may need to be honed off.

Question
Can a stone be re-polished once it has been sealed with a silicone impregnator?

Answer
Yes, because polishing affects only the surface of the stone.

Question

I have been told that our deteriorating marble building should have a consolidant applied. What is a consolidant, and how does it work?

Answer

Consolidants are materials applied to masonry and stone that bind the loose minerals of the stone or masonry together. Consolidants are used on stone that has been severely weathered and has lost its natural binding materials. The most common consolidants contain derivatives of silicone dioxide, a silicone-based material that penetrates into the stone or masonry surface. The consolidant locks itself into place, cures, and forms silicone dioxide, a glass-like material that binds and hardens the stone or masonry. *Note: Consolidants should only be applied by experienced professionals.*

Question

We have 12 men's restrooms, all containing a white Italian marble. We are having problems with urine stains at the base of all the urinals. What can we apply to the marble to keep it from staining?

Answer

There are numerous products on the market that repel water and oil. Unfortunately, urine is an acid, and currently there is no product on the market that repels acid. My advice would be to apply a good quality oil-repellent impregnator and to thoroughly clean the area on a daily basis with a solution of ammonia and water.

However, there are several companies working on an acid-resistant sealer for marble. Keep your eye out for them in the trade journals.

Question
Would you recommend applying a silicone-based impregnator to an historic limestone building?

Answer
First, make a determination of whether the building needs this kind of protection. Second, there are numerous environmental conditions that need to be assessed before you make that decision. Pollution, weather, region, current stone condition, moisture content, and other factors all need to be assessed before applying any protectant to any type of building.

Question
We cannot keep a shine on our green slate floor. It seems to scuff and mar continuously. We are currently using a high-speed acrylic wax. What can you suggest?

Answer
Unfortunately, scuffing and marring are a couple of the disadvantages of coatings such as the one you are using. You may want to try a coating that has a higher solids percentage. This may help reduce the scuffing.

Question
We are having trouble keeping the grout in our travertine floor clean. Can you recommend a sealer?

Answer
Most of the silicone impregnators on the market also work well as grout sealers. Thoroughly clean the travertine and the grout, and apply a good quality impregnator to the travertine and the grout.

Question

We have a tan marble floor that has several coats of polyurethane on it. We want to remove this coating and restore the stone to its original condition. However, the floor is located in a hospital, and we cannot use any chemical that has a noxious odor. What do you suggest?

Answer

There are several ways to remove polyurethane coatings without using chemicals with a strong odor. Space-age technology has arrived, and there are some new products on the market available for removing these coatings. Some have no odor at all. These chemicals usually are sold as safe strippers or non-methylene chloride strippers. Most are available at hardware and home centers. Follow the directions carefully. Unlike methylene chloride strippers, the dwell time required to remove the polyurethane is much longer.

Question

We are having a lot of trouble with hard water spots on our polished granite shower. Is there anything we can put on the granite to prevent these spots?

Answer

Yes. A good quality application of silicone impregnator should do the trick. It may also be helpful to install a water treatment system to reduce the calcium in the water.

Question

We applied a highly recommended oil-repellent impregnator to a marble floor in a hotel restaurant. The floor is still staining. What can we do?

Answer

The problem is more than likely not with the impregnator. Most impregnators are only oil-repellent, not oil-proof. If the oil is allowed to sit on the stone long enough, it will penetrate the stone and cause stains. Clean the floor more frequently, and try to clean up oil spills as soon as they occur.

Question
We have a polished granite floor that is extremely slippery. Is there any sealer we can put on top of it to increase its slip-resistance?

Answer
There are several sealers on the market that will increase the coefficient of friction (COF). Check with your local supplier, and be sure the product is recommended for stone.

CHAPTER 5

STAIN IDENTIFICATION

Before attempting to remove a stain, there are several steps that can be taken to identify its nature. This process can then help determine what methods can be used to remove the stain.

1. Is it a true stain?
    * Check for etching by feeling the stone. If it's rough, it's probably etched.
    * Check for efflorescence. Is there a white powder residue that easily wipes off?
    * Check for water spots or water rings. Remember that these are not stains and appear in the shape of rings or spots.
    * Check for stun marks, which are little white marks, usually numerous on certain marble. These marks can be very deep and difficult to remove.
    * Check to make sure the stone is not wet. A wet spot may look like a stain that will disappear when dry.

2. What color is the stain?
    Color can be a dead giveaway. Red or brown may indicate rust. See Table 5-1 for help on identification of stains by color.

3. Look and feel
   Does the stained area feel sticky? Does it feel wet? Does it feel rough or smooth? What pattern is the stain? Does it look like something spilled and have a splatter pattern?

4. Smell
   Smell the stained area. When all else fails, the olfactory senses can be your best detective tool. If the odor is sour, it may be a food stain. If the smell is pungent, it may be vomit or urine. If it smells like a solvent, it may be paint or a solvent-carried chemical. If it has no odor, go to Step 5.

5. Evidence
   Where is the stain? Carefully take a look around, and try to recreate how the stain may have occurred. Is the stain next to the refrigerator? Is there an animal in the house that may have had an accident? Has there been any recent remodeling? What type of traffic or use does the surface get?

Stain Color	Possible Stain
Black	Tar, asphalt, fungus, mildew, oil, grease, soot, ink, dirt, heel marks, shoe polish
Blue	Copper, ink, bronze, plant fertilizer
Brown	Algae, wood stain, coffee, tea, tobacco, dirt, grease, oil, paper, food, urine, chocolate
Gray	Aluminum, efflorescence, mortar, thinset, paper, soot, plants
Green	Bronze (Figure 5-1), copper, ink, algae, mildew, food, dyes
Orange	Rust, fruit drink, food
Red	Blood, rust, ink, food
White	Aluminum, efflorescence, etching, thinset, mortar
Yellow	Eggs, grease, mustard, rust, urine

Table 5-1. Stain identification color chart

When all else fails and you still have no idea what the stain is, treat the stain as outlined in Chapter 6, Unknown Stain Removal Procedure.

The above guidelines are not complete and are only intended as clues to the potential source of a stain.

Figure 5-1. Bronze staining of limestone due to bronze fixture

TROUBLESHOOTING

With the following tools and chemicals, almost all stains listed in this book can be removed. Use a large plastic tool box to carry the following items:

TOOLS
* Razor blades
* Paper towels
* Clean, white cloths
* Pencil eraser
* Empty spray bottle
* Scrub brush
* Diatomaceous earth
* Poultice powder
* Sponge

CHEMICALS
* Clean water
* Stone soap
* Neutral cleaner
* Ammonia

- 20% to 50% hydrogen peroxide
- Toluene
- Mineral spirits
- Hydrochloric acid
- Alkaline floor stripper
- Methylene chloride
- Commercial degreaser
- Gum freeze
- Acetone
- Denatured alcohol
- Digestive enzyme

STAIN REMOVAL AND TROUBLESHOOTING

Once a stain is clearly identified, the steps to remove it can begin. These should be followed in numerical order, and close attention should be paid to the warnings for certain situations.

Acne Creams

Types
Most acne creams on the market today contain benzol peroxide, a bleaching agent.

Problem
Acne creams that contain dyes can cause staining. These dyes are usually flesh-toned to brown in color.

Solution
1. Thoroughly clean the area with water and soap (a mild detergent).
2. Once the area has dried, take some acetone on a clean white rag and rub the stained area.
3. If the acetone doesn't work, poultice the area with a poultice powder and 30% to 50% hydrogen peroxide.

Adhesives

Types
Tape residue, cellophane, bandages, stickers, etc.

Problem
Adhesives will leave a sticky residue on the surface of stone. Some tape residues — especially duct tape — can penetrate below the surface of the stone and become very difficult to remove.

Solution
1. Peel off any remaining tape. Use a very sharp razor blade, and be careful not to scratch the surface of the stone.
2. The remaining sticky residue usually can be removed with a rag and acetone. Pour the acetone on a clean white rag, and rub the area until all of the sticky residue is gone.
3. If the adhesive has left a stain, prepare a poultice of diatomaceous earth or similar powder with one of the following solvents:

   ◇ Mineral spirits
   ◇ Toluene
   ◇ Xylene
   ◇ Methylene chloride

Several poultices may need to be applied to completely remove all staining.

Alkaline Etching

Types
Etching from alkaline strippers, ammonia, and heavy duty stone cleaners

Problem
Alkaline etching is caused by alkaline salts contained in cleaners, with the salts being deposited below the surface of the stone. The etch marks appear similar to an acid etch mark.

Solution
1. Attempt to remove the etching with a mild acid. If the stone is a polished marble, do not use acid.
2. If dealing with a polished marble, re-hone and re-polish the etch. If the etch appears light, try re-polishing only.

Aluminum

Types
All aluminum — usually from windows, awnings, etc.

Problem
Aluminum can leave a crusty, whitish residue.

Solution
1. On polished surfaces, scrape any crusty residue from the surface with a sharp razor blade. On textured surfaces, use a hard brush.
2. On textured surfaces, mix one part hydrochloric acid in 20 parts water, apply the solution, and agitate with a soft nylon brush.
3. On polished surfaces, dilute one part hydrochloric acid in 40 parts water, apply the solution, and agitate with a soft nylon brush. Re-hone and polish the surface to return the luster. *Caution: Be extremely careful with hydrochloric acids near marbles, because they will severely etch the surface.*

Beer

Types
There are literally hundreds of beers. Dark beers seem to cause more stains. Light-colored countertops are very susceptible to dark beer staining.

Problem
The sugars and proteins in the beer can cause a very dark stain on light-colored stones.

Solution
1. Clean the entire area thoroughly with water and a mild detergent (a dishwashing soap such as Ivory™ works well). Allow the water and soap to soak into the stone for several minutes. Lightly agitate the area, and remove excess water with a dry towel. Rinse the area with clear water.
2. If the above cleaning procedure does not remove the beer stain, try a stronger cleaner such as ammonia and water.
3. If the stone is still stained, prepare a powder poultice with 30% to 50% hydrogen peroxide. Several poultices may need to be applied.

Bleach

Types
Common household bleach, Soft Scrub™ with bleach, and mildew killers

Problem
Bleach contains sodium hypochlorite, which is an acid that can etch soft marbles. It may also lighten certain sedimentary stones like shell stone and coquina.

Solution
1. Flood the area with clean water to remove any excess bleach.
2. If the stone is etched, re-polish the area with a polishing powder such as aluminum oxide and oxalic acid. A pre-packaged powder is recommended. Apply a small amount of powder, add some water, and rub the area into a slurry with a white buffing pad.
3. If the stone has lightened, there is very little that can be done. A light application of linseed oil may cosmetically darken the area to help hide the discoloration.

Blood

Types
Human and animal blood; raw meats prepared on a marble countertop can cause blood staining.

Problem
Blood contains salts and proteins. If cleaned while still fresh, blood will usually not stain. If allowed to dry, blood stains can be very difficult to remove.

Solution
1. Clean the area thoroughly with cold water and a mild detergent.
2. Prepare a solution of 50% household ammonia and water. Apply this solution, and allow it to sit for several minutes. Gently scrub the area, and rinse with cold clear water.
3. If the stain is still present, poultice with a powder such as diatomaceous earth and ammonia.

Burns

Types
Cigarette, hot irons, propane, and others

Problem
Cigarette and cigar burns will leave a yellow nicotine stain, which can be difficult to remove. Cigarette burns can also melt the stone and in the case of granite, may cause spalling.

Solution
1. If the stone is melted or spalled, re-honing and polishing will be necessary.
2. If a yellow nicotine stain is the problem, poultice with 35% hydrogen peroxide and poultice powder.
3. If several hydrogen peroxide poultices do not work, try poulticing with powder and toluene.

Candy (non-chocolate)

Types
There are hundreds of types of candies — all containing sugar and various dyes.

Problem
Several candies contain dyes. Red dye is particularly difficult to remove.

Solution
1. Scrape remaining candy from surface.
2. Clean area with acetone and a clean white cloth.
3. If acetone doesn't work, poultice with powder such as diatomaceous earth and one of the following solvents:

   ◇ Mineral spirits
   ◇ Toluene
   ◇ Xylene
   ◇ Methylene chloride

Carpet Padding

Types
Carpet padding made of jute

Problem
Carpets that have jute backing can leave a difficult brown to yellow stain on stone surfaces. The jute is made of a burlap type material.

Solution
1. Scrape any excess carpet padding from the surface.
2. Clean the area thoroughly with a good detergent and clean cold water.
3. Poultice with 20% to 50% hydrogen peroxide and poultice powder.

Jute backing can cause some very deep stains that can penetrate throughout the stone.

Chocolate

Types
Candy, cocoa, ice cream, etc.

Problem
Chocolate can leave brown stains in light-colored marbles.

Solution
1. Clean the area thoroughly with cold water and a good detergent.
2. If the stain is still present, clean with ammonia and water. Let the solution sit on the stained area for several minutes. Remove the excess solution, and rinse with clear cold water.
3. If the above procedures fail, poultice with diatomaceous earth or a similar powder and ammonia. Difficult

chocolate stains may require poulticing with 20% to 50% hydrogen peroxide.

Coffee and Tea

Types
Instant coffee, hot tea, and iced tea

Problem
Coffee and tea both contain tannin, which can leave a yellow to brown stain, Figure 6-1. If left on stone long enough, the stain can penetrate deeply and be nearly impossible to remove. If the concentration of coffee or tea is strong enough, it can also etch the surface of polished marble.

Figure 6-1. Coffee stain on limestone

Solution
1. Pour 35% hydrogen peroxide directly on the stain, and add a few drops of ammonia. Leave until the bubbling stops. *Caution: Do not use ammonia only. Ammonia can permanently set the stain.*

2. If the above procedure does not remove the stain, poultice with powder and 35% hydrogen peroxide.
3. If all else fails try poulticing with toluene or xylene.

Copper

Types
Copper piping, sculptures, etc.

Problem
Copper can cause a green stain that can sometimes penetrate deep into the stone if allowed to age.

Solution
1. Remove any excess crust by scraping with a sharp razor blade. If the surface is polished, wet the surface with soap and water to prevent scratching the stone.
2. Prepare a solution of one part ammonia and three parts warm water. Apply this solution to the surface and agitate with a soft bristle brush. Rinse with clean water.
3. If the stain is still present, poultice with ammonia chloride and poultice powder. Ammonium chloride-based cleaners are available from chemical supply companies.

Crystallization

Type
Crystallization is a process used to polish marble (includes all brands).

Problem
If this process is overused, it can build up and turn yellow on light-colored stones. It also may give the stone a plastic look. Currently, this process is under great controversy and is being investigated and tested by the marble and stone care industry.

Solution
1. Crystallization can be stripped chemically using a solution of oxalic acid and water. Start by using one cup of oxalic acid to one gallon of water. Apply this solution to the stone and agitate with a hog's hair pad.
2. Once the coating is removed, re-honing and polishing will be necessary.
3. An alternative method to chemical stripping is to grind the crystallization off, re-hone, and re-polish.

Efflorescence

Types
A dry white powder on the surface of the stone. True efflorescence is loose and will wipe off easily.

Problem
Most conditions that cause efflorescence are water related. Efflorescence will continue to be a problem unless the moisture is eliminated.

Solution
1. Do not use any water, cleaners, etc., in an attempt to remove efflorescence. This will only cause more efflorescence.
2. Remove the efflorescence with a dry white cloth or buff using #000 steel wool. Wait to see if the efflorescence returns. If it does, repeat dry buffing.
3. If the efflorescence condition is indoors, it sometimes helps to install dehumidifiers or turn the air conditioner down to about 72°F.

It can take several months for the stone to dry completely.

Egg

Types
Chicken, duck, or other eggs

Problem
Eggs contains albumin, a protein which can leave a yellow stain, Figure 6-2.

Figure 6-2. Egg stain on limestone floor

Solution
1. Clean the area thoroughly with cold water and detergent (a commercial stone soap). *Caution: Do not use hot water, because it can set the stain.*
2. If the stain remains, poultice with poultice powder and 20% to 50% hydrogen peroxide.

Fruit and Juice (light)

Types
Apples, pears, oranges, lemons, limes, grapefruit, and their juices

Problem
The acids in some fruits, especially lemon, will etch polished marble. The sugars in these fruits will turn yellow or brown if allowed to sit too long.

Solution
1. If the surface is etched, re-polish using a commercial polishing powder. If the etch is very deep, re-honing may be necessary.
2. If the fruit has left a stain, clean the area with cold water and a good detergent.
3. If the stain still remains, poultice with poultice powder and 20% to 50% hydrogen peroxide.

Fruit (red)

Types
Cherries, grapes, blueberries, blackberries, cranberries, raspberries, strawberries, and their juices

Problem
All of these fruits contain dyes, which can be very difficult to remove.

Solution
1. Clean the area with cold water. *Caution: Do not use soap; it can set the stain.*
2. If the stain remains, poultice with 20% hydrogen peroxide and poultice powder.
3. If the stain is still not removed, poultice with toluene and poultice powder.

Furniture Polish

Types
Spray and liquid furniture polishes

Problem
Oils, dyes, waxes, and silicones can cause staining. The darker polishes such as walnut can permanently stain the stone.

Solution
1. Clean with acetone and a clean white rag. Allow the acetone to sit on the stained area a few minutes, and blot the remaining acetone with a clean rag.
2. If the stain is still present, poultice with one of the following solvents:

   ◇ Poultice powder
   ◇ Mineral spirits
   ◇ Toluene
   ◇ Xylene
   ◇ Methylene chloride

Glue (synthetic)

Types
Super glue, hot glue, epoxy resin, plastic model cement

Problem
These glues will rarely stain but are usually hard to remove from the surface.

Solution
1. On smooth surfaces, scrape glue with a sharp razor blade. Be careful not to scratch the surface.
2. Any remaining residue can be cleaned with acetone and a clean white rag.

3. If the glue is very stubborn, soak the area in acetone for several minutes and try scraping with a razor blade. Follow this by wiping with acetone.

Glue (water soluble)

Types
Casein, Elmers™, mucilage, paste, and hide glue

Problem
White and clear glues rarely stain. However, some of the darker glues can leave a stain that can be difficult to remove.

Solution
1. Scrape excess glue with a sharp razor blade. Be careful not to scratch the surface.
2. Clean with cold water and a good detergent. Try using a green scouring pad.
3. If the glue is stubborn, use acetone and a clean white rag.
4. If the glue has left a stain, poultice with toluene or a similar solvent and poultice powder.

Grass

Types
Typical lawn grass

Problem
Tannin and chlorophyll in grass can leave a green or yellow stain.

Solution
1. Clean the stained area with a clean white rag and denatured alcohol.
2. If the stain remains, poultice with 20% to 50% hydrogen peroxide and poultice powder. *Caution: Do not use*

*ammonia or any alkaline cleaners on grass stains. They
can permanently set the stain.*

Grease (food)

Types
Butter, margarine, fried foods, mayonnaise, salad dressings,
gravy, etc.

Problem
Fats and oils can leave a dark stain, which can be difficult
to remove. Some salad dressings and foods contain dyes,
which also can cause staining.

Solution
1. Thoroughly clean the stained area with cold water and
   a good detergent.
2. Apply a commercial degreaser to the stained area, and
   let it sit for several minutes. Remove excess degreaser
   and rinse with clean clear water.
3. If the stain is still present, poultice with commercial
   degreaser and poultice powder.
4. For stubborn stains, poultice with a solvent such as
   toluene and poultice powder.

Grease (other)

Types
Petroleum-type grease such as wheel-bearing grease,
cooking grease, vegetable oils, etc.

Problem
Grease can leave a dark stain that can penetrate deeply
into the stone and be very difficult to remove. Try to remove
the grease as soon as it is spilled.

Solution
1. Clean the area thoroughly with cold water and a good detergent.
2. Soak stained area with a commercial degreaser for several minutes. If the degreaser solution dries, reapply and keep it wet. Remove the excess degreaser, and rinse with clear water.
3. If the stain is still present, poultice with commercial degreaser and poultice powder.
4. For stubborn grease stains, poultice with toluene or methylene chloride and poultice powder.

Gum

Types
Chewing gum, tree gum (sap), etc.

Problem
Gum rarely stains stone surfaces but can be very difficult to remove from honed and rough textured surfaces.

Solution
1. Do not try to scrape gum off the surface, as this only makes more of a mess. Freeze the gum using an aerosol gum freeze, available at most janitorial supply houses. Spray the gum for several seconds, then chip it off with a scraper or putty knife. This should remove most of it.
2. If there is any gum residue remaining, apply a solvent cleaner such as a dry spotter, also available at most janitorial supply houses.

Hard Water Stains

Types
Water stains from irrigation systems, faucets, bathroom fixtures, or shower walls

Problem
The minerals in water will leave deposits that can appear as a white haze or large deposits of crust-like minerals.

Solution
1. If deposits are large, try scraping off excess deposits with a sharp razor blade.
2. Apply a solution of weak phosphoric acid, and agitate the area, applying more acid as needed. This will etch all marble surfaces, so plan on refinishing the marble.
3. Re-hone and re-polish the stone if necessary.

Some mineral deposits will be embedded below the surface of the stone and may cause spalling. If this is the case, replacement of the damaged stone is the only alternative.

Heel Marks

Types
Black rubber, neoprene

Problem
Heel marks can leave a black streak on the surface of stone. These are rarely stains but can be difficult to remove from rough textured stones.

Solution
1. Clean with acetone and a clean white rag. On textured stone, try using a green scrub pad with acetone.
2. If acetone doesn't work, try another solvent such as a dry spotter, available at janitorial supply houses.

Ice Cream (not chocolate)

Types
All flavors except chocolate

Problem
Food coloring and fruits can cause staining.

Solution
1. Clean the area thoroughly with cold water and a good detergent.
2. If the stain remains, poultice with 20% to 50% hydrogen peroxide and poultice powder.
3. If the stain is very stubborn, try a poultice with toluene or a similar solvent and poultice powder.

Ink

Types
Ball point pen, permanent marker, carbon paper, newspaper print, etc.

Problem
Most inks penetrate deeply into the stone and can be very difficult or nearly impossible to remove, depending on the age of the stain. It is very important to get to the stain as quickly as possible.

Solution
1. Clean the area thoroughly with acetone and a clean white rag.
2. Poultice the stain with a solvent such as toluene or methylene chloride.

Several attempts will be necessary to remove the stain. If no improvement is noticed after five attempts, the stain is most likely permanent.

Iodine

Types
Iodine, mercurochrome, and similar dyes found in medicines

Problem
They can leave a stain that can be nearly impossible to remove.

Solution
1. Blot any wet iodine with a clean white rag.
2. Clean the area with denatured alcohol and a clean white rag. Be sure to blot the area. Do not wipe, this will only make the stain larger. Blot until you see no more dye on the white rag.
3. If the stain still remains, poultice with denatured alcohol and diatomaceous earth or similar poultice powder.

Jam and Jelly

Types
All types and flavors (artificial and natural preserves)

Problem
Dyes and fruits can cause staining, especially grape and berry jams and jellies.

Solution
1. Clean the area thoroughly with cold water and a good detergent.
2. If the stain remains, poultice with a toluene or equivalent solvent and poultice powder.

Juice (powdered)

Types
Fruit drinks and popsicles, etc.

Problem
Dyes can be difficult to remove, especially the red and orange types.

Solution
1. Clean with a solution of ammonia and water. This will help neutralize the dye.
2. Poultice with a commercial remover made especially for this type of stain (available at janitorial supply houses) and poultice powder. Removers such as Kool Off™, Red Out™, and Stain Away™ work well.

Leather

Types
Shoe and clothing leather

Problem
Leather contains oils and dyes, which can penetrate into stone and cause staining.

Solution
1. Clean the area thoroughly with acetone and a clean white cloth.
2. If the stain is deep, poultice with a solvent (toluene) and poultice powder.

Lipstick

Types
All colors and types

Problem
Oil, waxes, and dyes can be difficult to remove, Figure 6-3.

Figure 6-3. Lipstick stain on limestone floor

Solution

1. Scrape excess lipstick with a sharp razor blade. Lipstick is very concentrated, and attempting to clean without scraping the excess will only spread it around.
2. Once all the excess is removed, clean with acetone and a clean white rag.
3. If the stain is still present, poultice with a solvent such as toluene and poultice powder.

Liquor

Types
Mixed drinks and white wine; not red wine or beer

Problem
Alcohols can melt agglomerate-type stones. Dyes can cause staining.

Solution

1. Agglomerate stones that are damaged can sometimes be filled with a polyester resin. Seek professional help if this is the case, or replace the stone.
2. Stains will need to be poulticed with a solvent such as toluene and a powder poultice.

Lotion

Types
Baby lotion, body lotion, suntan lotion, hair oil, etc.

Problem
Lotions contain various oils and can cause dark staining. They can be difficult to remove if left on too long.

Solution

1. Thoroughly clean area with water and a good detergent.
2. Prepare a solution of a commercial degreaser and water. Apply the solution to the stained area, and let it sit for several minutes. Agitate and remove the excess solution, and rinse with cold clear water. Repeat several times.
3. If the stain is deep, apply a poultice of commercial degreaser and poultice powder.

Makeup

Types
Mascara, blush, eye shadow, liquid foundation, etc.

Problem
Dyes, waxes, and oils can stain stone. Most makeup has a high concentration of dye, which can be tricky to remove.

Solution

1. Remove any excess makeup by blotting with a clean white rag. Do not wipe, as this will only spread the stain.

2. Clean the stained area with denatured alcohol and a clean white cloth. Blot, do not wipe.
3. If the stain remains, poultice with 20% to 50% hydrogen peroxide and poultice powder.
4. If the stain still remains, poultice with a solvent (toluene) and poultice powder.

Mildew

Types
Mildews, fungus, algae, and other living plant stains

Problem
These plants can leave a black, green, blue, orange, or white blotchy stain on stone surfaces. Since these plants are living, they can grow and spread at a rapid rate, usually requiring a moist environment to grow.

Solution
1. Clean area thoroughly with a good detergent.
2. If there is any soap film on a shower wall for example, be sure to remove the soap film by scraping and then wiping with a clean rag and acetone.
3. To remove the mildew, spray the area with a solution of three parts household bleach, one part water, and several drops of dish detergent. Continue to mist the area until all mildew disappears.
4. Rinse the entire area with clean water and dry.

Milk

Types
Milk, cream, and other milk products

Problem
The animal fat contained in milk can sour and leave a yellow stain. It can also give off a bad odor.

Solution
1. Clean the area thoroughly with a good detergent.
2. Apply a solution of three parts bleach to one part water. Let it stand for several minutes, then rinse with clean water.
3. If the stain is still present, poultice with 20% hydrogen peroxide and poultice powder.

Mortar and Thinset

Types
Concrete, thinset, mudset, grout films, and other concrete-based residues

Problem
These substances can leave a film on the surface of the stone that can be hard to remove. Concrete will very rarely stain unless it is colored.

Solution
1. If the film is light, clean the surface of the stone with a heavy duty stone cleaner (available from stone care suppliers) and water.
2. If the film is stubborn, clean the surface with a solution of one part hydrochloric acid to 20 parts water on textured stone and one part hydrochloric acid to 40 parts water on polished stone. Agitate until the mortar is removed.
3. Re-hone and re-polish marble surfaces. *Caution: Hydrochloric acid can severely etch polished marble.* **Use extreme caution.**

Mud

Types
Mud, dirt, red clay, etc.

Problem
Most dirt is not a big problem. However, red clay can leave stains that can be difficult to remove.

Solution
1. Clean area thoroughly with a good detergent and plenty of cold water. This should remove all surface dirt.
2. If the dirt has left any stains, poultice with household ammonia and poultice powder.
3. If the stain was caused by red clay and the ammonia does not remove it, poultice with a mixture of one part laundry detergent (Tide™ works well) and two parts poultice powder.

Mustard

Types
All types

Problem
Mustard contains turmeric, which is a yellow spice that causes the yellow staining. Mustard stains can be very difficult to remove, especially if the stain is old.

Solution
1. Thoroughly clean the stained area with cold water and a good detergent. Blot only.
2. Pour 20% to 50% hydrogen peroxide directly on the stain and add a few drops of ammonia. Leave until the bubbling stops.
3. If the stain is still present, poultice with 20% to 50% hydrogen peroxide and poultice powder. *Caution: Do not use ammonia or alkaline-type cleaners on mustard stains unless you like the color of mustard.*

Nail Polish

Types
Enamel or lacquer types

Problem
Nail polishes dry very quickly. For this reason, the dyes contained will rarely penetrate into polished stone. Rough texture stone is another problem. The nail polish will penetrate immediately, causing a difficult stain.

Solution
1. Immediately blot with a clean white cloth.
2. Apply acetone to the stain and blot with a clean white cloth. Continue to apply acetone and blot until the stain disappears.
3. If the stain is old, poultice with a solvent (toluene, alcohol, etc.) and a poultice powder such as diatomaceous earth.

Oil

Types
Automotive, cooking, and lubricating oils, etc.

Problem
Oil can be very difficult to remove on most stones. Oils will penetrate deeply into the stone and will spread throughout. Try to clean up the oil spill as soon as it happens.

Solution
1. Blot any excess oil with a clean white cloth. If the oil has dried on the surface, scrape with a sharp razor.
2. If the oil is still fresh and has penetrated into the stone, sprinkle a generous portion of dry poultice powder on the spill and let stand for 12 to 24 hours.
3. Remove the dry poultice, and prepare a solution of commercial degreaser and water. Apply this solution to

the spill, and keep it wet for 30 minutes. Vacuum the solution, and blot the remainder with a clean white cloth.
4. If the stain is still present, poultice with a solvent (methylene chloride works best) and a poultice powder such as diatomaceous earth.

Paint (oil based)

Types
All oil-based paints and alkyd resins and solvents

Problem
Oil-based paints are the most difficult paints to remove. The oils and solvents contained in these paints will carry the dyes deep into the stone, Figure 6-4.

Figure 6-4. Spray paint stain on limestone floor

Solution
1. Immediately blot any excess paint from the surface with a clean white cloth.

2. Apply liberal amounts of mineral spirits (paint thinner) to the spill and blot. Continue to blot until no color is observed on the cloth.
3. Apply a poultice of methylene chloride or a commercial paint remover and a poultice powder.

Paint (water based)

Types
All water-based paints and polymer resins

Problem
These are not as difficult to remove as oil-based paints but can still cause severe headaches trying to remove.

Solution
1. If the spill is fresh, blot immediately with a clean white cloth.
2. Clean the area with water and a good detergent.
3. If the stain is dry, scrape the paint with a sharp razor blade. If scraping is difficult, apply a solution of soap and water to the spill and scrape while wet.
4. If the stain has penetrated the stone, poultice with a commercial water-rinseable paint remover and poultice powder.

Paper

Types
Brown paper bags and construction paper

Problem
It is very common for contractors to cover a new stone floor with brown construction paper. If this paper gets wet or slightly wet, it will bleed into the stone and leave an ugly brown stain.

Solution
1. Clean the area with acetone and a clean white cloth.
2. Poultice the area with a solvent (mineral spirits or toluene) and poultice powder.

Pencil

Types
Graphite and indelible pencil

Problem
Pencil can be tricky to remove, since the graphite may penetrate into the stone. Commonly, the pencil mark is only on the surface of the stone.

Solution
1. Try taking an eraser and erasing the mark. This procedure works almost 90% of the time.
2. If the pencil mark has penetrated the stone, poultice with denatured alcohol and poultice powder.

Perfume

Types
Oils, alcohol, and fragrances

Problem
Oils can penetrate the stone and cause a light oil spot. Alcohols can also react with certain stones and turn a brown color.

Solution
1. Clean the area thoroughly with denatured alcohol and a clean white cloth.
2. If the stain is deep, poultice with denatured alcohol and poultice powder.

Perspiration

Types
Body oils, salts, and enzymes

Problem
Oils from perspiration are a big problem on walls, countertops, and other areas where hands are constantly touching the surface of the stone.

Solution
1. Blot the area with denatured alcohol and a clean white cloth.
2. If the stain is still present, poultice with denatured alcohol and poultice powder.

Pet Stains

Types
Urine and vomit

Problem
Urine and vomit contain acids which can etch polished marble. The proteins they contain can also stain the stone and have a terrible odor.

Solution
1. Try to clean up the accident as quickly as possible. Blot the area with a clean white cloth.
2. Apply a solution of one part vinegar, one part 35% hydrogen peroxide, and six parts water. Let the solution soak into the stain for several minutes, and pick up with a wet vacuum.
3. After treatment, apply a solution of a commercial bacteria/enzyme digester (available at janitorial supply houses). Cover with a paper towel soaked with digester. Allow to sit overnight. This should remove the odor. It may require several applications of digester to remove the odor.

Rust

Types
Iron oxide

Problem
Rust is one of the most difficult stains to remove. It can cause a reddish-brown to yellow stain that can permanently set into the stone.

Solution
1. If the rust is new, try applying a solution of Iron-Out™ (available at home centers) and water. Mix into a slurry, and lightly agitate the area with a soft bristle brush. Rinse with clear water. *Caution: This product may cause etching. Be prepared to re-polish.*
2. If the stain is old and has penetrated into the stone, poultice with Iron Out™ and poultice powder. *Caution: Do not use clay powders; instead, use diatomaceous earth.*
3. If this does not work, poultice with hydrofluoric acid and poultice powder. *Caution: Never use bleach. It will only make the stain worse.*

Shoe Polish

Types
All liquid polishes including white polish

Problem
Dyes in shoe polish can penetrate the stone, leaving a stain, Figure 6-5.

Figure 6-5. Shoe polish on limestone floor

Solution
1. If dry, scrape the excess polish with a clean sharp razor. Apply a solution of stone soap to help lubricate the blade and prevent scratching.
2. Clean the area thoroughly with acetone and a clean white cloth.
3. If the stain still appears, poultice with a solvent (e.g., toluene) and a poultice powder.

Silicone

Types
Silicone caulking used for grouting and anchoring stone

Problem
This can be a serious problem when caulking is used to help hold anchors in place on stone wall panels. The silicone will start to bleed through the stone in the areas where the anchors are located. It may take several months before the silicone becomes visible.

Solution
The only known technique that will remove silicone staining is to prepare a poultice with methylene chloride (commercial paint remover) and a powdered poultice. It may require a dozen applications. If the silicone has not completely cured, the staining may return again.

Smoke or Soot

Types
Smoke and soot from fireplaces and fire damage (does not include tobacco smoke)

Problem
Smoke and soot contain particles of oil and carbon, which can leave a black ugly mess.

Solution
1. Wipe the excess soot with a clean, dry, white cloth.
2. Clean the area thoroughly with a solution of stone soap or dishwashing soap in warm water. Use a stiff bristle brush for rough textured stone.
3. If the smoke damage is heavy, clean with a solution of commercial degreaser (available at janitorial supply houses) and warm water.
4. If smoke damage is still present, poultice with commercial degreaser and poultice powder.

Soap Film

Types
Soap film on shower walls and vanity tops

Problem
Soap from showers can build up on shower walls, leaving a film that will not wash off with regular cleaning.

Solution

1. If the soap film is thick, scrape with a razor blade. Wet the surface to avoid scratching the surface.
2. Once all heavy build-up is removed, clean with acetone and a green scrub pad.
3. There are also commercial soap film removers on the market that work well, but be sure they do not contain acids, which can etch polished marble.

Soft Drinks

Types
All carbonated sodas

Problem
The coloring and sugars in sodas can cause severe staining, Figure 6-6.

Figure 6-6. Soft drink stain on limestone floor

Solution
1. If the spill is fresh, blot with a clean white cloth.
2. Clean the area thoroughly with a good detergent and warm water. Flood the stained area thoroughly.
3. If the stain is still present, poultice with 20% to 50% hydrogen peroxide and poultice powder.

Soups

Types
All soups and stews containing meat and vegetables

Problem
Soup and stew can leave greasy stains that can be difficult to remove, especially if the stain is old.

Solution
1. Clean the area thoroughly with a solution of ammonia and water.
2. If the area is stained after cleaning, poultice with ammonia and poultice powder.
3. If the stain is still present, poultice with 20% to 50% hydrogen peroxide and poultice powder.

Soy Sauce and Worcestershire Sauce

Types
All brands of soy and Worcestershire sauces

Problem
Coloring and proteins in these sauces can be extremely difficult to remove.

Solution
1. Clean the area thoroughly with acetone and a clean white cloth. Be sure to blot only.
2. Poultice with a solvent (toluene, etc.) and poultice powder.

Streaking

Types
All types of streaking, appearing as a cloudy uneven pattern on the surface of the stone

Problem
Streaking can be caused from the following:

- Dirty mops used to mop floors
- Improper application of waxes and coatings
- Improper cleaners
- Too much cleaner

Solution
1. Determine what is causing the streaking, and eliminate the cause.
2. If the streaking is caused by wax build-up, strip the surface with a commercial wax stripper (available at janitorial supply houses).
3. If the streaking is caused by too much cleaner, a dirty mop, or improper cleaner, re-mop the floor with stone soap and buff with a white nylon pad.

Stuns

Types
Stun marks caused by heavy objects dropped on a marble floor or high heel shoe marks

Problem
Stun marks are very common on some marbles, usually caused from women walking across the floor with high heels, which may leave a white spot on the marble. Stun marks can telegraph to the bottom of the stone. They are caused from the individual crystals in the stone exploding, Figure 6-7.

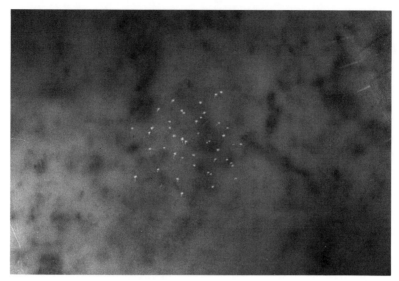

Figure 6-7. Stun marks on white marble

Solution
Try grinding, honing, and polishing the floor. This may eliminate some light stuns, but chances are they cannot be removed.

Swirls

Types
Circular pattern swirls

Problem
Swirl marks appear as circular patterns on the surface of the stone. They are usually caused by floor machines using abrasive pads, such as steel wool, that have trapped sand and grit under them.

Solution
Light swirls can be removed by re-polishing. Heavy swirls will require re-honing and re-polishing. *Caution: When*

using any type of rotating machine (floor buffer, automatic scrubber, and/or hand machine) never hold the machine still while running. Always keep the machine moving. Keeping the machine still may cause severe swirling.

Syrup

Types
Honey, molasses, maple syrup, and corn syrup

Problem
The sugar and coloring added to these syrups can cause staining.

Solution
1. Thoroughly clean the stained area with cold water and a good detergent.
2. If the stain remains, clean with ammonia and water. Let the solution sit for several minutes, then agitate and rinse with clean water.
3. If the stain is still present, poultice with 20% to 50% hydrogen peroxide and poultice powder.

Tar

Types
Asphalt, roofing tar, beach tar, etc.

Problem
Dyes in tar can cause deep staining in stone.

Solution
1. Scrape away any excess tar with a clean dry razor blade.
2. Clean the remaining tar with acetone and a clean white cloth.
3. If the stain remains, poultice with mineral spirits (i.e., paint thinner) and poultice powder.

4. If the stain is stubborn, poultice with De-Solv-It™ (available at hardware stores) and poultice powder. *Caution: Do not use water with tar. It will harden the tar and set the stain.*

Tire Marks

Types
All types of tire marks created by cars, trucks, carts, etc.

Problem
These vehicles can leave rubber tracks on stone surfaces. Rarely will tire marks stain, but they can be difficult to remove on porous surfaces such as rough stone, concrete, or brick.

Solution
1. Clean thoroughly with a commercial degreaser and warm water. Scrub with a stiff bristle brush.
2. If the marks are stubborn, clean with a solvent (mineral spirits or toluene). Use a stiff bristle brush.

Tobacco

Types
Smoke stains from cigarettes and cigars

Problem
Nicotine can cause a light yellow stain that can be difficult to remove, Figures 6-8 and 6-9.

Figure 6-8. Tobacco smoke discoloration on marble walls

Figure 6-9. Tobacco smoke discoloration removed from marble walls

Solution
1. Clean the area thoroughly with a good detergent and cold water.
2. For heavy tobacco stains, clean with a commercial degreaser and cold water.
3. If the stain remains, poultice with a commercial degreaser and poultice powder.

Tomato

Types
Canned or fresh tomatoes, tomato pastes, juice, etc.

Problem
Acids in tomato products can etch the surface of polished marble. Tomatoes can also leave a red stain in porous stones.

Solution
1. Clean the area thoroughly with cold water and a good detergent. Rinse with clear water.
2. If the stone is stained, poultice with 20% to 50% hydrogen peroxide and poultice powder.
3. If the stone is etched, re-polish with polishing powder.

Tomato-Based Sauces

Types
Barbecue, steak, and spaghetti sauce, ketchup, etc.

Problem
These sauces contain tomato, tannin, oil, and dyes. The dyes will leave a red to brown stain. The oil will penetrate the stone, making it darker.

Solution
1. Clean the area thoroughly with cold water and a good detergent.

2. If the stain is still present, clean the area with an alkaline degreaser (commercial degreasers are available at most janitorial supply houses). Mix with water according to the directions, and let the solution stand on the stained area for several minutes. Agitate with a cloth, and rinse with clean water.

3. If the stain is still not removed, poultice with powder (diatomaceous earth or similar powder) and an alkaline degreaser. A second poultice may be required using powder and a solvent such as toluene or methylene chloride if dye is present.

Toner

Types
Copy machine toner and similar inks

Problem
This is one of the most difficult ink stains to remove. If the stain is allowed to sit, it may become permanent.

Solution
1. Thoroughly clean the area with acetone and a clean white cloth. Continue to clean until no ink is transferred to the cloth.

2. If the dye has penetrated the stone, poultice with methylene chloride (commercial paint stripper) and poultice powder.

Vegetables

Types
Green and yellow vegetables

Problem
These vegetables will leave a green-yellow stain on stone surfaces.

Solution
1. Clean the area thoroughly with a good detergent and cold water.
2. If the stain is still present, poultice with 20% to 50% hydrogen peroxide and poultice powder.

Vomit

Types
Human or animal vomit

Problem
The acids in the stomach have a very low acidic pH and can severely etch the surface of polished marble. They also can leave a stain, depending on what was eaten.

Solution
1. Clean the area thoroughly with a good detergent and cold water.
2. Clean the area with a solution of household ammonia and cold water. Continue cleaning until the stain is completely gone.
3. If the stain is still present, apply a poultice of ammonia and poultice powder.
4. If odor remains, apply a solution of enzyme digester (available at janitorial supply houses). Keep the area wet for several hours (covering with a wet paper towel will help).
5. If stone is etched, re-polish with polishing powder.

Water Rings/Spots

Types
Rings from drinking glasses and hard water spots from drips

Problem

Water usually will not stain but will leave a white ring or spot. This ring or spot is made of deposits of minerals from the water. If the drink contains acid (lemon in iced tea), it will etch polished marble in the shape of a ring or spot.

Solution

1. Try buffing the ring or spot with dry #000 steel wool.
2. If the ring or spot still remains, re-polish with polishing powder.
3. If the ring or spot is very deep, re-honing may be necessary. *Caution: If the stone has been waxed or colored with dyes, the ring may have cleaned the wax or dyes from the surface. To test for waxes or dyes, take some acetone and clean an inconspicuous area. If the stone lightens, there is a wax or dye on the stone. If this is the case, you will need to re-wax or re-dye.*

Waxes/Coatings

Types

Waxes, acrylics, urethane, epoxy, etc.

Problem

Waxes can yellow and give a plastic appearance. They will also attract dirt.

Solution

1. If the coating is water based (acrylic), strip the stone with a commercial wax stripper (available at janitorial supply houses). Be sure to rinse thoroughly.
2. If the coating is solvent based (waxes, urethane, epoxy), strip with a commercial paint stripper containing methylene chloride. There are also non-methylene chloride strippers available that work effectively on these materials.
3. Once all the coatings have been stripped, re-honing and re-polishing may be necessary.

Wine

Types
All red wines

Problem
The tannin contained in red wine can severely stain stone, Figure 6-10.

Figure 6-10. Wine stain on limestone floor

Solution
1. Clean the area thoroughly with acetone and a clean white cloth. *Caution: Do not use detergent and water, as this may set the stain.*
2. If the stain is still present, poultice with 20% to 50% hydrogen peroxide and poultice powder.
3. If the stain is stubborn, try poulticing with a solvent (toluene) and poultice powder.

Wood Stains

Types
All solvent-based stains and dyes

Problem
The dyes contained in these stains can be nearly impossible to remove (they are designed to stain wood). The older the stain gets, the harder it is to remove.

Solution
1. Clean the area thoroughly with acetone and a clean white cloth. Continue to clean until no stain is visible on the rag.
2. Prepare a poultice with methylene chloride (commercial paint stripper) and poultice powder. It may take several attempts to pull these difficult stains out.

Yellowing

Types
General yellowing across the surface of most stones, especially white marbles

Problem
There are many causes for yellowing of stone. For example, UV light can cause yellowing over time; iron contained naturally in stone can oxidize and cause yellowing; inexpensive coatings can cause yellowing; and mastic used to set stone can turn yellow.

Solution
If the yellowing is caused by iron contained naturally in the stone or the stone is aging, you will never get it out. Natural yellowing of white marble, particularly the Carrara types, is very common and cannot be reversed at this stage. If the yellowing is caused by waxes or coatings, strip them off according to stripping directions.

UNKNOWN STAIN REMOVAL PROCEDURE

The following procedure is to be used only if you have no indication of the stain type. Be sure to test this procedure before applying it to the entire area.

1. Remove the excess stain material from the surface by scraping with a very sharp razor blade.
2. Blot the stain with acetone and a clean white cloth. If the staining material transfers to the white cloth, continue blotting until no additional stain is transferred. Proceed to Step 6. If no stain is transferred to the white cloth, proceed to Step 3.
3. Clean the area thoroughly with cool water and a good stone soap or neutral cleaner. Use a white cloth to remove the excess solution. If stain is transferred to the white cloth, proceed to Step 7. If the stain is not transferred, proceed to Step 4.
4. Blot the area with 20% hydrogen peroxide and a clean white cloth. If the stain material transfers to the white cloth, continue blotting until no stain is transferred. Proceed to Step 8. If no stain is transferred, proceed to Step 5.
5. Clean the area thoroughly with an iron removing cleaner (Iron-Out™ or equivalent). Agitate with a soft brush or cloth, and remove the excess with a white cloth. Be careful, as most iron-removing chemicals contain acids and may etch the stone. If the stain is lightened proceed to Step 9. If the stain is not changed by this method, proceed to Step 10.
6. Apply a poultice using diatomaceous earth or an equivalent powder and one of the following solvents (in order from mild to strong): mineral spirits, toluene, or methylene chloride. Several poulticings may be needed, but use only one solvent type. Don't mix solvents. Continue to poultice until the stain is removed. If stain is not removed or lightened after five attempts, proceed to Step 10.
7. Apply a poultice of diatomaceous earth or equivalent powder and an alkaline stone cleaner or heavy duty neutral cleaner. Several poultices may need to be

applied. Continue to poultice until the stain is removed. If the stain is not removed or lightened after five attempts, proceed to Step 10.

8. Apply a poultice of diatomaceous earth or equivalent and 20% hydrogen peroxide. Do not use clay or earth powders with hydrogen peroxide. If the stain is difficult to remove, re-poultice using 50% hydrogen peroxide. Several poultices may need to be applied. Continue poulticing until the stain is removed. If the stain is not removed or lightened after five attempts, proceed to Step 10.

9. Apply a poultice with diatomaceous earth or equivalent and an iron-removing chemical (Iron-Out™ or equivalent). Continue poulticing until the stain is completely removed. Re-honing and/or re-polishing may be necessary on marble. If the stain is not removed or lightened after five attempts, proceed to Step 10.

10. If the stain is not removed, chances are it has become permanently set or it is part of the stone. Replace the stone or live with the stain. A throw rug works very well in these situations.

CHAPTER 7

MATERIAL SAFETY DATA SHEETS (M.S.D.S.)

WHAT IS A MATERIAL SAFETY DATA SHEET?

A Material Safety Data Sheet (M.S.D.S.) is a form that must be supplied with every chemical that may be considered hazardous. The M.S.D.S was developed by the Occupational Safety and Health Administration (OSHA) as part of the Hazardous Communication Standard (HAZCOM). It was developed to provide one easy reference for hazardous substances.

There is no single correct M.S.D.S. form, and many companies will produce their own forms. No matter what style of form, they all must contain the same information, which includes the following:

- Chemical trade name
- Name of the manufacturer or distributor
- Address of the manufacturer or distributor
- Why the chemical may be hazardous
- How you can be exposed to the hazardous chemical
- What conditions can cause the chemical to become more hazardous
- How to safely handle the hazardous chemical
- What type of protection is required when using the chemical
- What you need to do if exposed to the chemical
- What to do if you spill the chemical

All manufacturers, distributors, importers, and suppliers are required to distribute an M.S.D.S. for every hazardous chemical they distribute. In addition, all employees working with hazardous chemicals must have access to the information provided on the M.S.D.S.

You don't have to be a chemist to read and understand an M.S.D.S. The information on an M.S.D.S is very important and should not be ignored. The M.S.D.S. is divided into nine sections as follows:

Identification
The identification portion of the M.S.D.S. contains the following information:

- The name of the chemical — usually the product trade name
- The name and address of the manufacturer or distributor
- An emergency telephone number
- Trade names and synonyms
- The date that the M.S.D.S. was written or the date that any changes were made

Hazardous Ingredients Identity Information
The hazardous ingredients portion of the M.S.D.S contains the following information:

- The chemical names, formulas, and common names of hazardous ingredients
- OSHA permissible exposure limits — the maximum amount of the chemical a person may be exposed to without harm
- The threshold limit value (TLV) — the amount of the chemical a person can be exposed to for five consecutive eight-hour workdays without harm

- The chemical abstracts service (CAS) identification number
- Other recommended limits

Sometimes you will find a chemical in this section that is labeled a *trade secret*. The M.S.D.S. will still list its hazards and safety information without identifying the chemical.

Physical and Chemical Information

This portion of the M.S.D.S. contains the following information:

- Boiling point — This is the temperature at which a liquid will boil. This information will help you prevent a potentially dangerous change in state. When a liquid reaches its boiling point, it turns into gas. The liquid may be safe, but as a gas the chemical may be deadly.
- Vapor pressure — This measures a liquid's tendency to evaporate. The higher the vapor pressure, the faster the liquid will evaporate.
- Vapor density — This tells us if the liquid is heavier or lighter than air. If heavier than air, it will settle on the ground; if lighter than air, it will rise.
- Solubility in water — If a chemical is not soluble in water, do not mix it with water. An example of a liquid that is not soluble in water is mineral spirits.
- Appearance and odor — This will help you recognize the chemical and alert you to possible danger.
- Specific gravity — This tells us if the chemical will sink or float in water. If over 1.00, it will sink. If less than 1.00, it will float.
- Melting point — This is the temperature at which a solid changes to a liquid.
- Evaporation rate — This is the temperature at which the chemical evaporates. If the chemical has a high evaporation rate, you would not want to store it in a hot place.

Fire and Explosion Hazard Data

This portion of the form contains the following information:

- Flash point — This is the temperature at which a chemical or substance will ignite if exposed to a spark or flame. If the flash point is 90° to 120°F, the fumes can be ignited by a cigarette, electrical equipment, etc. If this is the case, store these chemicals in a cool area where no smoking is permitted.
- Flammable limits — This is the concentration of the chemical in the form of a gas or vapor that is needed for it to ignite if exposed to a spark or flame.
- Extinguishing media — This information explains what to use to put out a fire caused by the chemical. Sometimes the extinguishing media will be classified as follows:
  - Class A — Paper, wood, straw, and cloth — These can be fought with water.
  - Class B — Flammable and combustible liquids — These can be fought with carbon dioxide, foam, or dry chemicals.
  - Class C — Fires caused by electrical equipment — These can be fought with carbon dioxide or dry chemicals.
  - Class D — Combustible metals — These require special extinguishing compounds.
- Special firefighting procedures — This will indicate if any special materials, equipment, or methods are needed to fight this type of fire.
- Unusual fire and explosion hazards — Any unusual fire or explosive nature of this chemical will be listed here.

Reactivity Data

This portion of the form contains the following information:

- Stability — This will indicate conditions such as heat, pressure, or shock to be avoided when storing, using, or transporting the chemical.

- Incompatibility — This will tell which chemicals or conditions to avoid.
- Hazardous decomposition — When the chemical decomposes, it may release certain hazardous products which will be listed in this section.
- Hazardous polymerization — This indicates what happens when this chemical comes into contact with other chemicals which could cause a problem.

Health Hazard Data

This portion of the M.S.D.S. contains the following information:

- Route(s) of entry — This indicates how the chemical can enter the body (breathing it in, through the skin and eyes, or by being swallowed).
- Health hazards — This will indicate the long- and short-term effects of the chemical on the body.
- Carcinogenicity — This will indicate if the chemical can cause cancer.
- Signs and symptoms of exposure — This indicates what signs to look for if exposed to this product (appearance, headaches, dizziness, nausea, etc.).
- Pre-existing medical conditions that are aggravated by exposure — This tells you to avoid the chemical because of respiratory problems, allergies, kidney and liver problems, etc.
- Emergency first aid procedures — These tell you what to do in case of an accident with the chemical.

Spill or Leak Procedures

This portion of the form contains the following information:

- What to do if you spill the chemical or if it leaks
- How to dispose of the chemical and its waste
- Other precautions characteristic of this chemical

Special Protection Information

This portion of the M.S.D.S. contains the following information:

- Respiratory protection — Is a mask or respirator needed?
- Ventilation — Does the area you are working in need to be exhausted?
- Are protective gloves required, and if so, what kind (vinyl, rubber, etc.)?
- Eye protection — Are safety glasses or goggles needed?
- Other protective clothing and equipment needed

Special precautions

This final portion of the form contains the following information:

- Precautions to take in handling or storage
- Other precautions

Don't take the information contained on the M.S.D.S. lightly. It contains important information that you and your workers must know before using, handling, or storing the chemical. When you buy a chemical, request its M.S.D.S. You must be provided with one if you ask for it; it's the law.

Figure 7-1 is an example of the M.S.D.S. for acetone.

```
┌─────────────────────────────────────────────────────────────────────┐
│                    MATERIAL SAFETY DATA SHEET                         │
│                  (Prepared According to 29 CFR 1910.1200)             │
│                                                                       │
│ Date Prepared        October 3, 1994                                  │
│                                                                       │
│ SECTION 1 — PRODUCT IDENTIFICATION                                    │
│ Distributor Name: ABC CHEMICALS CO.                                   │
│ Emergency Telephone No.: 000-000-0000                                 │
│ Address: ANYTOWN, USA                                                 │
│                                                                       │
│ Trade Name: ACETONE                                                   │
│ Chemical Family: KETONES                                              │
│                                                                       │
│ SECTION 2 — HAZARDOUS INGREDIENTS                                     │
│ Chemical Name/Common Name      Cas No.     Percent      TLV(Source)   │
│ ACETONE                        67-64-1     100%         750           │
│ DIMETHYL KETONE                                                       │
│                                                                       │
│ SECTION 3 — PHYSICAL DATA                                             │
│ Boiling Point (°F): 133°F     Specific Gravity (H₂O = 1.0): .7905   pH: N/A │
│ Vapor Pressure (mm Hg): 186 mm Hg     Vapor Density (Air = 1): HEAVIER │
│ Solubility in Water: COMPLETE                                         │
│ Evaporation Rate (vs H₂O): LESS THAN 1                               │
│ Appearance and Odor: CLEAR, SHARP ODOR                               │
│                                                                       │
│ SECTION 4 — FIRE AND EXPLOSION HAZARD DATA                           │
│ Flash Point: 0°F                                                      │
│ Extinguishing Media: CARBON DIOXIDE OR DRY CHEMICAL, ALCOHOL TYPE     │
│                      FOR LARGE FIRES                                  │
│ Special Fire Fighting Procedures: SELF CONTAINED BREATHING APPARATUS  │
│                                   WITH POSITIVE PRESSURE              │
│ Unusual Fire and Explosion Hazards: KEEP AREA FREE OF HOT METAL       │
│                                     SURFACES AND SOURCES OF IGNITION  │
│                                                                       │
│ SECTION 5 — REACTIVE DATA                                             │
│ Stability: STABLE          Incompatibility: AVOID CATALYST SUCH AS    │
│                                            SODIUM HYDROXIDE           │
│ Hazardous Decomposition Products: BURNING CAN PRODUCE CO AND CO₂      │
│                                                                       │
│ SECTION 6 — HEALTH HAZARDS                                            │
│ Threshold Limit Value: SEE SECTION 2                                  │
│ Primary Route of Exposure: Eye_x_ Skin_x_ Oral_x_ Inhalation_x_ Other__ │
│                                                                       │
│ SECTION 7 — EMERGENCY AND FIRST AID PROCEDURES                        │
│ Eyes: Flush immediately with water. Obtain medical attention if severe irritation occurs. │
│ Skin: Flush with water.                                              │
│ Ingestion: Induce vomiting.                                          │
│ Inhalation: Move to fresh air. If not breathing, give artificial respiration and seek │
│             medical attention.                                       │
│                                                                       │
│ SECTION 8 — SPECIAL PROTECTION INFORMATION                           │
│ Respiratory Protection: Use in well ventilated area.                 │
│ Ventilation Requirements: Local exhaust_x_ Mechanical_x_ Other__     │
│ Protective Gloves: Rubber gloves        Eye Protection: Safety glasses │
│ Other Protective Clothing: Impermeable apron                         │
│                                                                       │
│ SECTION 9 — SPILL OR LEAK PROCEDURES                                 │
│ Steps to be taken if Released or Spilled                             │
│ Waste Disposal Methods: Follow Federal, State, or Local laws for disposal of solvents. │
│                                                                       │
│ SECTION 10 — STORAGE AND HANDLING INFORMATION                       │
│ Keep container tightly closed. Keep product cool, dry, and away from sources of ignition. │
└─────────────────────────────────────────────────────────────────────┘
```

Figure 7-1. Sample M.S.D.S. for acetone

GLOSSARY

A

ABSORPTION COEFFICIENT
A value given to determine the rate at which a stone will absorb a liquid.

ACID
A water soluble chemical with a pH less than 7. Some typical acids are hydrochloric, hydrofluoric, acetic, sulfuric, phosphoric, and oxalic. Refer to Chapter 2 for further information on acids.

AGGLOMERATE
A stone type composed of many pieces of stone held together with polyester or similar resins.

ALKALINE
A water soluble chemical with a pH greater than 7. Some typical alkaline chemicals are ammonia and sodium hydroxide. Refer to Chapter 2 for further information on alkaline chemicals.

ANCHORS
Rods, pins, or other devices used to hang stone on a vertical surface.

ATTEAPULGITE
A type of clay powder used for poulticing stains from stone. Refer to Chapter 1 for further information.

B
BULL NOSE
A convex rounding of a stone tile or slab; typically found on a counter or vanity top.

C
CALCIUM CARBONATE
The main mineral found in most marble.

CAULKING
An elastic adhesive or plastic polymer used to seal the joints of stone.

COATING
A protective layer applied to the surface of stone. Waxes, floor finishes, acrylics, and polyurethanes are all coatings designed to provide protection, waterproofing, and luster.

CRYSTALLIZATION
A term used to describe a marble polishing process. It is sometimes called recrystallization or vitrification. Refer to Chapter 4 for further information.

D
DIATOMACEOUS EARTH
A powder type used for poulticing stains from stone. Refer to Chapter 1 for further information.

DIGESTIVE ENZYME
A chemical that contains an enzyme that will digest certain odor causing bacteria.

E

EFFLORESCENCE
A deposit of salts found on the surface of stone carried by moisture from the setting materials. Efflorescence appears as a white powder residue.

ETCH
A rough, dull mark produced by acid eating away at a polished surface.

EXPANSION JOINT
A joint between stone designed to expand and contract to prevent cracking of the stone.

F

FABRICATE OR FABRICATION
To construct or shape stone into another shape. For example, to cut a stone slab into a table top is to fabricate a table top.

FILLING
The filling of holes and cracks in stone with cements, plastic resins, or shellac.

FINISH
The final surface applied to the face of the stone. A wax or coating may also be called a finish.

FRACTURE
A fault or failure in a stone producing a break in the stone.

FULLERS EARTH
A clay used for poulticing stains from stone.

G

GROUT
The material used to fill in the joints between stone tile. Grout can be cement or plastic resins.

GUM FREEZE
A product used to spray on chewing gum, freezing it, so that it can be removed.

H

HEARTH
The floor part of a fireplace on which the fire is placed.

HONED
A term used to describe a smooth surface finish on stone or the process of achieving the finish.

HYDROPHOBIC
Water repelling; typically used to describe the properties of certain sealers used to impart water repellence to stone.

I

IGNEOUS
A geological term used to describe a type of stone formation. Granite is an example of an igneous stone.

IMPREGNATOR
Term used to describe a stone sealer that penetrates the stone surface and does not form a coating. An impregnator is often referred to as a penetrating sealer.

INORGANIC
Term used to describe substances composed of matter other than plant or animal. Minerals are inorganic.

J
JOINT
The space between stone panels or tiles. Referred to as a grout joint.

K
KAOLIN
A type of clay used for poulticing stains from stone.

L
LIPPAGE
A term used to describe uneven tiles; i.e., when one tile is higher or lower than the adjacent tile.

M
METHYL CELLULOSE
A powder type used for poulticing stains from stone. Refer to Chapter 1 for further information.

MORTAR
A mixture of cement, lime, sand, and water. Mortar is often used as a setting bed for tile.

MOSAIC
The setting of small tiles in a pattern or a picture.

M.S.D.S.
An abbreviation for Material Safety Data Sheet (see Chapter 7).

N
NEUTRAL CLEANER
A water based cleaner with a pH of 7. Used for daily cleaning of tile and stone surfaces.

O

OLEOPHOBIC
Oil repelling; used to describe the properties of certain sealers used to impart oil repellence to stone.

ORGANIC
A substance derived from living organisms (plant or animal). Stains such as food are organic in nature.

OXIDIZE
To change a compound by increasing its electronegative change. When iron turns to rust, oxidation of the iron takes place.

P

PENETRATING SEALER
Term used to describe a sealer that penetrates the stone surface. A penetrating sealer does not form a coating. Also called an impregnator.

pH
The measure of the acidity and alkalinity of a solution. Numbers are assigned from 1 to 14. Seven indicates a neutral pH, neither acid nor alkaline. Numbers lower than 7 are acid, and numbers higher than 7 are alkaline.

POINTING
The filling of joints between stone tiles or panels. Also referred to as grouting.

POULTICE
A powder or cloth placed on a stain, which is designed to remove the stain by absorption.

Q

QUARRY
The name given to the place where stone is removed from the ground.

R

RECRYSTALLIZATION
The term used to describe a marble polishing process. Also called crystallization or vitrification. See Chapter 4 for further information.

S

SEPIOLITE
A powder type used for poulticing stains from stone. Refer to Chapter 1 for further information.

SETTING
The act of installing stone or tile.

SLAB
A slice of stone produced by sawing a large block of stone.

SOLVENT
A liquid substance capable of dissolving other substances. Although water is considered a solvent, the term solvent generally refers to waterless substances.

SPALL
The condition that results when the stone surface splits or is broken off.

STONE SOAP
A stone cleaner containing soaps made from vegetable oils.

STUN
Term used to describe the white mark that results from the striking of a sharp object against certain stone.

T
TEXTURED
A pattern produced on the surface of a stone.

TOOLED
A pattern produced on the surface of a stone with a tool or hammer.

TREAD
The top walking surface of a step.

V
VEIN
The colored markings in stone.

VITRIFICATION
A term used to describe a marble polishing process. It is sometimes called crystallization or recrystallization.

W
WATER SPOTTING
The spot produced on a stone surface from the sprinkling or dropping of water.

WAXING
The application of a wax finish to the surface of a stone or the filling of natural voids in stone.

WEATHERING
The wearing of a stone surface resulting from elements of the weather.

INDEX

Other Titles Offered by BNP